SOUL STORIES

BY GARY ZUKAV

The Seat of the Soul

Thoughts from The Seat of the Soul:
Meditations for Souls in Process

The Dancing Wu Li Masters:
An Overview of the New Physics

GARY ZUKAV

SOUL
STORIES

SIMON & SCHUSTER
A VIACOM COMPANY

First published in Great Britain by Simon & Schuster UK Ltd, 2000
A Viacom Company

3 5 7 9 10 8 6 4 2

Simon & Schuster UK Ltd
Africa House
64–78 Kingsway
London WC2B 6AH

Simon & Schuster Australia
Sydney

A CIP catalogue record for this book is available from the
British Library

ISBN 0-7432-0908-7

Printed and bound in Great Britain by The Bath Press

*To my daughter Jenifer
and my granddaughter
Jamie, with love
and wonder.*

Contents

Contents

Contents

PART IV

How It Happens

SOUL STORIES

Introduction

This is a book of true stories. Sometimes I have used the real names of the people in them, and sometimes I have used other names. Sometimes I have told the story exactly the way it happened, and sometimes I have combined stories into one. Sometimes, the stories are not about things that actually happened, but those stories are true, too.

The Lakota people, who are Native Americans, have a story about the white buffalo calf woman. She is the one who gave them their sacred pipe. A reporter asked a Lakota elder one day if he thought that the story of the white buffalo calf woman was true. The elder said, "I don't know whether it actually happened that way or not, but you can see for yourself that it's true."

Introduction

You can see for yourself that all of the stories in this book are true, too. You have to look inside yourself to do that. Every Soul Story, whether you find it in this book or somewhere else, requires that you look inside yourself to see if it is true. You may find that something that is true for someone else is not true for you. You might also find that something that is true for you is not true for someone else. That is the way that it is with Soul Stories.

For example, some people say that the universe is dead (they call it "inert"), and that everything that happens is accidental (they say "random"). Other people, like me, say that the Universe is alive, wise and compassionate. Looking at the universe as dead is one story. Looking at it as alive is another. Which story is true for you?

You have to decide. Each of the Soul Stories in this book gives you an opportunity to decide whether it is true for you or not. The Lakota elder said that you can see for yourself when a story is true, but before you can do that, you have to know about it. That means thinking about it and, even more important, discovering what you feel about it. Eventually, you might find that what you feel about a Soul Story is more important to you than what you think about it.

You can read all of the Soul Stories in a few days, or you can choose one here and there when you feel like it. Since there are fifty-two of them, you can also read one each week to give yourself time to consider each one. That way you will be thinking about Soul Stories for an entire year. Even if you read them all the first day, you can still read them again, one each week, to give yourself a little more time with each story.

Introduction

I love Soul Stories. For me, every story that makes me appreciate myself and you, and that makes me happy that we are together, even when things get very difficult, is a Soul Story. Every story that makes me appreciate the Earth, and look at it as a great Friend, is a Soul Story, too.

I am happy to share these Soul Stories with you.

Love,

Gary

PART I

What's New

Multisensory Perception

It was a gray winter afternoon. The black, sleek car was traveling fifty miles an hour when it hit the ice. Like a graceful dancer, it began a slow, horizontal pirouette as it slid toward a steep embankment and then disappeared over it. Inside, a young woman screamed as the car rolled again and again like a ball careening downward and spinning at the same time. That woman was my sister.

One hundred miles away, an older woman with gray hair suddenly rose out of her chair.

"Something has happened to Gail!" she gasped.

The telephone rang forty minutes later.

"Your daughter has been in an accident. She is not hurt badly, but her car was destroyed."

How could this have happened? The woman who rose in alarm, my mother, could not see her daughter struggling for her life as the car crashed again and again against the frozen ground and, at last, into a barren tree. She could not smell the crushed bushes beneath the battered car, or the gasoline from the ruptured tank. She could not hear the bending of metal and the shattering of glass, feel the impact of the car as it tumbled, or taste the blood in her daughter's mouth.

She did not have to. She used multisensory perception. Multisensory perception is a direct link with information that the five senses cannot provide. It eliminates the distance between the one who knows and what she knows. It eliminates the time between them. My mother did not need to wait for the police to tell her that her daughter's life had been in danger. She knew it as clearly as if she had watched, heard, smelled, felt, and tasted the experience herself. She engaged another way of knowing.

The businessman was late for his plane. He waited impatiently for his ticket, and then drove quickly into the huge airport garage. The first level was full. So was the second. Up and up he spiraled, one narrow ramp after the other, becoming more worried each moment. Level three was full, and so was level four. As he approached the ramp to the last level, desperate now, he suddenly stopped. A large sedan came speeding around the curve, going the wrong way. Neither would have seen the other before the crash.

How did he know that car was coming? He could not see it, hear it, or smell it. His ability to taste and touch could not help him. This is also an example of multisensory perception. *Multi* means more than one. Taste, touch, smell, hearing, and sight are different ways of sensing, but they are all part of a single system. That system is designed to detect one thing—the world that appears to be outside of you. If you only have five senses to navigate, you are limited to this system.

When the brochure first came in the mail, the woman did not give it much attention. It was about a conference that was too far away, too expensive, and not about the things that were most interesting to her. The next day, she felt an impulse to read it again, and the next day, too. She could not put it out of her mind, nor the curious feeling that she should attend. Without knowing why, she registered and booked a flight. The first day there she met a man who was struggling with cancer. She had a passionate interest in the healing process. With her assistance, his cancer disappeared, and they coauthored a book on healing.

Where did her impulse come from? She had two systems to provide her with information. The first—her five senses—didn't give her information about what might happen at the conference. Another system did. That second system is multisensory perception.

My friend Jeffrey had come to a dead end. He wanted to study "deviant personalities" from a positive point of view—what makes some people more fulfilled and happy than others. His graduate program in criminology only studied them from a negative point of view—what makes some

23

people more violent than others. One night he dreamed that he visited the house of two friends (whom he actually knew). They were not home, so he let himself in. On a table in the living room he found a magazine called *Eye.* It told him exactly what he needed to know.

The next morning, he hurried to tell his friends about this dream. They weren't home. He knew where they kept the key, so he let himself in, although he had never done that before. On a table in the living room he found a magazine called *Focus,* which included a schedule of programs on a national public television station. As he looked through it, he suddenly realized that he could study positive "deviant personalities" by interviewing them on television! He did just that. He called his program "Thinking Allowed."

Jeffrey's dream told him how to find what he needed. So did the woman's impulse to go to the conference. The businessman's hunch told him what he needed to avoid. These are examples of multisensory perception. Jeffrey, the woman, and the businessman listened to their multisensory perception. That is why Jeffrey has his television program, the woman is the coauthor of a book, and the businessman stayed out of the hospital.

Having multisensory perception and using it to help you are different things. This is important to realize because we are all becoming multisensory. If you understand that, you will be looking for ways to use this ability. Actually, this ability is not new. What is new is that everyone is now getting it.

In the past, we called this ability by another name.

Intuition

Have you ever been thinking about a friend when the phone rings?

"I was just thinking of you!" you exclaim. "What a coincidence."

The word *coincidence* means that two events happen at the same time, like your thinking about your friend and your friend's call. When this happens, it is never an accident. Your friend and you are connected in ways that your eyes, ears, nose, skin, and tongue cannot show you, but that your intuition did.

Have you ever had a feeling you shouldn't do something, and then did it anyway?

"I *knew* I shouldn't have trusted him!" you say.

That is right. You knew. Your intuition told you, but

you wanted so much to trust that you ignored what it told you.

Multisensory perception and intuition are the same thing, but multisensory perception is a more accurate name. Most people think that intuition is a hunch that occurs now and then, like the one the businessman had to stop his car, and the feeling the woman got about the conference. It is more than that. It is a very sophisticated system that allows you to see more than you can with your five senses. As we become more and more intuitive—and we all are—we encounter different kinds of these experiences.

Libby was my favorite grandmother. I loved to visit her when I was little. She had twin beds that folded out from the same sofa. We talked late every night, she lying on one bed, and I on the other.

There was a restaurant in Grandmother Libby's building, and after dinner we would walk through the lobby hand in hand. Each time she met a friend, she would say, "This is my grandson. You remember him, don't you?" I was terribly embarrassed when she did this, but if I objected (which I always did) she would jerk my hand downward and say, "Shuuuuush!"

I was in college when she died. A lot of people came to her funeral. When the rabbi gave her eulogy, I watched him from an alcove to his left. A small television hung from the ceiling. This gave us a frontal view of the rabbi. Seeing Grandmother Libby's funeral on television was so bizarre to me that I started to laugh. Suddenly I felt Grandmother Libby jerk my hand downward.

"Shuuuuush!" she said sharply.

She didn't want me disturbing her funeral. I stopped laughing and we stood silently, side by side, for the rest of the service. I never grieved Libby's departure because she didn't leave. I did not tell my family about this experience for thirty years. I didn't think they would believe me. Now that we are all becoming multisensory, it is not necessary to wait thirty years before sharing experiences like these. They are multisensory perceptions.

We can't see anything that is not physical with our five senses. Almost everything is nonphysical. That is why becoming multisensory is life-changing. It allows us to see what is nonphysical as well as what is physical. Everyone's life is now changing in this way. We are becoming more aware of intuition. We have more to pay attention to. The businessman didn't have to stop before the last ramp, but he saved himself a lot of trouble by doing so. The woman did not have to attend the conference, but she wouldn't have met her colleague, and his cancer might have taken a different course, if she hadn't.

There is no single way to experience intuition. It is different for everyone. Do you know anyone who is exactly like you—who weighs the same, has the same color hair, and the same length arms? Even if you have an identical twin, does he get sick when you do and like the same foods? Does she like the same music? That is not possible, because each of us is different.

The same is true of intuition. Some people have hunches. Some get ideas. Some people hear music, and others see pictures. Some people get sensations, like the feeling of a crisp, winter day. Others hear words. Some have conversations, as I did with Grandmother Libby. Some have combinations of these. None is the correct, or the only, way.

You can find your way by paying attention to what is happening inside you. This is the biggest difference between five-sensory perception and multisensory perception: The five senses require you to pay attention to what is outside of you. Intuition requires the opposite—that you pay attention to what is happening inside of you.

Using Intuition

The water was emerald and turquoise green—so clear that I could see each grain of sand beneath my feet. It gently lapped a beach that stretched as far as I could see. There were no surfers here. There was no surf. Linda, my spiritual partner, was floating faceup, with only her nose above the water.

I knew what she was doing. With her ears beneath the surface of the gentle ocean, she was listening. That is why we came to the beach every day, and why we came to Maui during the winter—to float in the healing water and listen.

I joined her and listened, too. The first thing I heard was my breath, but when I stopped breathing, I could hear faint sounds. First a soft clicking, and noise like sonar from a ship. Then a chirping noise. If I hadn't been listening so carefully, I would not have heard anything.

When I took a breath, I couldn't hear the sounds anymore, but when I held my breath again, they were still there. (They were often there, but I had been to Hawaii many times before I took the time to listen for them.)

I stood up. A school of dolphins was passing.

"There they are!" I shouted to Linda.

They were jumping out of the water as they swam, like children playing in the sun. I felt happy watching them, and it seemed to me that they were happy, too.

It was very exciting for me to see the dolphins so close, but Linda and I had come to listen for something else. I put my head back into the water and held my breath again. A low-pitched sound, like a melody from the moon, or a great moaning in the ocean, filled in the spaces between the sounds of the gentle waves breaking on the beach! Then other, higher-pitched melodies, and more low-pitched voices joined in. It was like listening to a symphony from space. The humpback whales were singing!

I didn't know how far away they were because sounds travel so well underwater, but it didn't matter. I could hear them clearly. These great creatures that swim the oceans as though they were hometown neighborhoods were back. No one knows exactly what their songs mean. Some people think they are a language that the whales use to talk to each other over thousands of miles. Others think they are music. Some think they are both. To me they are reminders of the greatness of Life, how little I know about it, and how special it is.

We floated and listened until we were full of the mystery and richness of their melodies. Then we left, already looking forward to coming again the next day.

Listening to your intuition is like listening for the whales. It is there, if you take the time to listen for it, and if there isn't so much noise that you can't hear it. I couldn't do anything about the ocean. It was calm most of the days we came to listen for the whales, but it isn't always that way. Once we came to Maui after a storm, and the waves were taller than I am. When that happens, I can't even get in the water. Days later, even when the waves were much smaller, they made too much noise for me to hear the whales.

When you are angry, your emotions are like huge waves on Maui during a storm. You cannot hear your intuition. When you are sad, or jealous, or vengeful, you can't hear your intuition, either. These emotions are too turbulent. Trying to hear your intuition when you are upset is like trying to hear a friend on the phone when people in the room are dancing to loud music, or cheering a ball game on the television. Your friend is speaking, but you can't hear her.

Even when you can't hear, your intuition is always telling you things that are helpful. Sometimes you can hear it even when you are agitated, like the businessman, but if you are trying, you can hear it more often. Imagine hearing your intuition every moment. You can do that, but you have to train yourself.

First, don't go to bed angry. This may take some work, but it is worth it. Your intuition works best when you feel light. Anger is heavy. It is a big load to carry. If you have it on your shoulders when you go to sleep, it will still be there when you wake up. When you let your anger go, you lighten up. That's when you open up, too. The same is true for every painful emotion—regret, guilt, shame, jealousy, and all the rest of them. Let them all go before you sleep.

Second, clean up your diet. Alcohol, caffeine, sugar, and tobacco cause violent storms in your body. The less you use them, the better your inner weather becomes. Meat and poultry are bloated with hormones, antibodies, and chemicals. None of them is put there for your health, and none of them is healthy for you. Eat fresh and light, and that is the way you will feel. (Everyone is becoming multisensory, not just vegetarians, but why not make it easy for yourself while you are learning?)

Third, believe that you have intuition, and believe that it works. This is very important. You can't stop your intuition from working, but you can keep yourself from hearing it. Believe that when you ask a question, you always get an answer. The answer may not come when you think it should, or in the way that you expect. It may come that night in a dream. It may come the next day, or the next week, in a conversation with a friend. You may have to take a walk or drive into town before you can relax enough to hear it, but an answer will always come.

Last, listen to what your intuition tells you. A lot of people hear answers that they don't like, so they pretend that they didn't hear any answers at all.

This brings us to a very interesting question. If your intuition can give you answers that you don't like, where do those answers come from?

Nonphysical Teachers

The Stockholm airport was smaller than I expected. Within minutes I was through customs and looking into the smiling eyes of my host, Ian.

"Welcome to Sweden!" he said, beaming as he greeted me. "Our car is waiting."

As I settled into the backseat for the long ride, he talked excitedly.

"They are all here—Saab, Volvo, SAS, the phone company, the banks—every major industry. This will be the best conference I have ever created. I am so glad you have come. We are all looking forward to your talk."

I was not. I could barely keep my eyes open. The long flight had been exhausting, but not so much as the month before in the desert. I struggled to stay awake. My life was upside down. I had no idea what I would say, or even if I would be able to speak. In four hours we arrived in central Sweden at a small, elegant hotel surrounded by woods.

"I have a surprise," Ian said mysteriously. "I want you to meet the inspiration for this conference."

Before I could say anything, he took my copresenters and me to a small room. At one end a middle-aged Swedish man sat in a chair. After greeting us through an interpreter, he closed his eyes, seemed to go to sleep, and then suddenly opened them again. His appearance had changed, and so had everything about him.

"Welcome," he said, through the interpreter. "I am Ambres."

"Ambres" was not the name of the man who had closed his eyes.

Oh, no! I thought. I am too tired for this.

I had seen "channeling" on television. I was not impressed. I did not believe in "nonphysical beings," and I didn't want to listen to one (even though I had watched Grandmother Libby's funeral with her twenty years earlier).

The next day Ian approached me at breakfast.

"You can speak with Ambres anytime," he said, smiling.

I took him up on his offer because, although I disdained "nonphysical beings," I did not want to miss the opportunity to experience one close up. When I saw Ambres again, only the interpreter and I were present.

"How did you learn to interpret your dreams?" Ambres asked me.

I was shocked. How could Ambres know what had happened to me in the desert? Yet that is exactly what I had done.

Ambres knew everything—the pain that had driven me into the desert, and what I had experienced there. He knew what I had seen, and how it had affected me. I made another appointment with him, and another. Each time we talked about my experiences in the desert, which I had not been able to explain, even to myself.

"A flame has been ignited in you," Ambres said, "but it is a small flame in a very large place, like a cathedral. You need to feed the flame, or it will go out."

"How do I feed the flame?" I asked.

"You talk to people," he replied.

"But Ambres," I exclaimed, "that is what I cannot do! If I talk to people, I may lose what I learned."

"Yes, you may fall," he said softly, "but if you do not feed the flame it will go out anyway. You must talk to people," he repeated. "The love that you give to them is the love that they will give to you. That is how you feed the flame.

"Can you do that?" he asked, looking into my eyes.

I thought for a moment. "Yes," I said. "I will try."

"Take my hands," he said, holding them out to me, "and I will be your witness."

(I learned later that the conference was on decision-making.)

I still did not believe in "nonphysical beings," but the only person who understood what had happened to me, and what was happening, was just that. I continued to question everything about Ambres, and to look for tricks.

"Why," I asked during our next meeting, "can't you talk to me directly? Why do you need an interpreter?"

"I can," replied Ambres, "but could you hear me?"

I am grateful for my skepticism because it left no doubt in me that whatever Ambres is, he is wise and he is a friend. Ambres was the first nonphysical Friend that I met, but he was not the last. Do you stop meeting friends after you have met one that is special? Of course not. I didn't, either. Having friends is the greatest joy in the Earth school. Becoming multisensory allows you to have more of them. It is like moving from a small town to a city. There are many more people and, because of that, more friends to meet.

Not everyone meets nonphysical Friends the way that I met Ambres. Some can listen better than I could in Sweden. They do not need "channels," much less interpreters. Everyone experiences nonphysical Friends in his or her own way. Some people hear voices. Some feel a presence. Others see pictures.

We usually think that hearing a voice, feeling a presence, or seeing pictures that others cannot hear, feel, or see happens only to people who are not well. When everyone was five-sensory, that was natural to think. Now everyone is becoming multisensory. There are still people who hear, feel, and see things that others cannot, and who are not well. The difference is that these people do not take responsibility for themselves. They think they must do what the voices inside them say. This is a very big difference.

Nonphysical Teachers do not tell you what to do. They help you see your options. They help you think through your choices. They help you understand what you are feeling, and why. They help you become more loving. They guide you to the fullest use of your life. You are still the boss. You still decide what is best for you, and what is not. You may talk a decision over with friends, but when it comes time to make it, it's up to you. That's the way it is with nonphysical Teachers. They are Friends who share with you. Then you decide what to do.

Everyone has a nonphysical Teacher. The more your life influences other people, the more nonphysical Teachers you have. A person who lives in a remote village does not require as much assistance as a person who influences millions, such as Mother Teresa or Gandhi. The more people your life influences, the more assistance you have available to you.

Having nonphysical Friends is now a part of being healthy, not sick. As you become multisensory, you will meet nonphysical Friends in your own way. Try this for a start. When you are about to say something, or do something, that you are not sure you want to say or do, ask yourself, "What is my motivation?" You will always get an answer. You may not like the answer you get, or get it when you expect, but an answer will always come. Then you can decide for yourself what to say or do.

This is how nonphysical guidance works. You ask. Then you listen. Then you decide.

When you check your motivation, you automatically engage nonphysical guidance. It's that simple. Try it and see what happens.

When you do, you will discover that you are experimenting with something very, very big.

Nonphysical Reality

The minivans pulled to a stop in front of the building. Doors swung open and out poured children, their teacher, and an assistant. Like flowers they colored the sidewalk, laughing and talking.

"Come, children!" said the teacher, "the professor is waiting."

Up the stairs they went, through doors, and into a room where a kind-looking man sat behind a table.

"Welcome," he said stiffly.

The long-awaited talk with a real scientist had begun.

"What do you do?" asked a boy in a blue shirt.

"I study radiation," answered the professor.

"What's that?" asked the boy.

"That's light," said the professor.

"Like from a flashlight?" asked a girl in a yellow dress.

"Yes," said the professor, "and more. Light that you can see is part of a continuum."

No one knew what to say.

"Do you know what a continuum is?" the professor asked.

They all shook their heads, "No."

The professor took off his glasses.

"It's something that doesn't have a beginning and doesn't have an end."

"Then where does it start?" asked a small girl with blond hair.

"That's the point," said the professor. "It doesn't start and it doesn't end."

No one said anything.

The professor tried again.

"A continuum is a spectrum. Who knows what that is?"

"It's red, orange, yellow, and blue," said the boy with glasses.

"And green and violet," added a boy beside him.

"It's a rainbow!" shouted a little girl.

"Exactly," said the professor. "A rainbow is a spectrum, but it is only a part of a bigger spectrum."

Again, no one spoke.

He tried a third time.

"Violet is at one end of the rainbow, isn't it? Violet has a lot of energy. That means it has a 'high frequency.' Take my word for it.

"Red," he continued, "is at the other end of the rainbow, isn't it? Red doesn't have much energy. It has a 'low frequency.'"

Everyone was listening.

"But some light has a frequency that is even lower than red. It's called infrared."

"That keeps the chickens hot," squealed a little girl.

The professor knew that she was thinking about her neighborhood deli.

"Exactly," he said. "And some light has a frequency even lower than that. There is always light with a lower frequency. It is part of the whole spectrum, too."

"Are there other parts?" asked a little boy.

"There are *always* other parts," said the professor. He held up a picture of a rainbow.

"This is the part of the light spectrum that you can see, but the whole light spectrum is bigger. How much bigger?" he asked no one in particular.

No one could say.

"Bigger than you can imagine!" he answered himself.

"It goes past red in this direction," he said, pointing his finger to the right. "Forever! It goes past violet," he continued, pointing his finger in the other direction. "Forever! That's what the whole light spectrum would look like if you could see it, which you can't."

The professor had hit his stride. He was no longer the stiff man behind the table.

"When I turn on a television," he said dramatically, "where does the picture come from?"

"From television waves?" asked a girl with glasses.

"Yes!" said the professor. "And where are those waves?"

"In this room?" said the little girl again, hesitantly.

"Exactly!" said the professor. "Exactly."

That is the way it is with nonphysical Teachers. They are in the room, too. Your eyes can't see television signals, but that doesn't mean they aren't around you. If you could see everything that is around you, you would see much more than your eyes can see.

The light that your eyes can see is part of the whole light spectrum, and that spectrum that doesn't have a beginning and doesn't have an end. The Universe is like that, too. It doesn't have a beginning, and it doesn't have an end. Everything that your five senses can detect has a beginning and an end, but the Universe doesn't.

Now we are becoming able to see a little more of the Universe. This is multisensory perception. It is like being able to see above violet into ultraviolet, or below red into infrared. We are beginning to see past the limitations of the five senses, and into nonphysical reality. That is why we are becoming aware of nonphysical Teachers.

You can't see television signals until you get a television, even though they are in the same room with you. Nonphysical Teachers are always in the same room with you. Becoming multisensory is like getting a television. It allows you to become aware of nonphysical Teachers.

It also allows you to become aware of something else.

Your Soul

When a fleet of ships sets sail, one of them sets the course for all of the others. It is the heart of the entire fleet, no matter how many ships are in it. Setting the course for the fleet does not mean determining what happens aboard each ship. The many interactions on each ship unfold in their own ways. People discover problems, and they work them out or they don't. They support each other or not. On some ships, the journey is generally pleasant. On others, it is always difficult.

Imagine that the mother ship is the largest seagoing vessel that you can picture in your mind—larger than the biggest ocean liner. It is an enormous city afloat. Imagine that the rest of the ships in the fleet are small boats, each with enough room for only one person. The mother ship is your soul, and you are one of the small boats.

You do not have the information that your mother ship has available to it. It is traveling on a vast ocean. You are temporarily part of its fleet. It was sailing before you came into being—before you were born—and it will continue its journey when your life is done. Yet your mother ship knows everything that happens to you. It knows every difficulty that you encounter, and how you handle it. It knows when the sea is calm for you, and when it is rough. In a way, you are a miniature of the mother ship. Although you are tiny compared to it, you are able to draw upon all of its capabilities if you are in communication with it.

When you are in touch with your mother ship, you have another, much larger perspective to guide you through the storms of your life. There is a reason that you are at sea, and a reason for the storms that you encounter. You cannot see those reasons, but, from the perspective of your mother ship, they are clear. You must make each of your decisions and experience what each of them creates. Your mother ship will not override your authority. Yet why flounder in high seas when you have a mother ship to assist you? It will not pull you out of the water, but it can help you to see things that you cannot see by yourself.

Your mother ship is the reason you are at sea. You were not forced to be a sailor. You volunteered. Through the decisions that you make, your mother ship, itself, is changed, or not. Your mother ship has its own destination. It always sails toward harmony, cooperation, sharing, and reverence for Life. When that is your destination, too, you are coordinated with it most effectively. If you sail in an opposite direction, you can lose track of it completely. Then you do not have your mother ship to help you. It was designed for the long haul. You were not. Your purpose is to learn how to sail most effectively with your mother ship.

We are each small boats with a mother ship, sailing on an ocean without a beginning and without an end. The small boats are temporary. The mother ships are not. When your life ends, you stop being a small boat, and become your mother ship. That is what you were before you became a small boat, and that is what you will be again. While you are a small boat, your job is to learn how to travel in the same direction that your mother ship is sailing. You are not the first small boat that your mother ship has put into the water, and you may not be the last. In short, you are part of a grand voyage, even though you, yourself, can see only a small part of it. When you become your mother ship again, you will see much, much more of it.

Meanwhile, your mother ship is always attempting to communicate with you. It does not communicate with satellites or computers. It uses your intuition. This is the same system that you use to communicate with nonphysical Friends and Teachers. Your intuition is like a radio that can receive signals from different stations. Some are nonphysical Teachers. Others are fellow souls. Another is your own soul.

Communicating with your own soul gives you a glimpse of the most fulfilled, wise, compassionate, and intelligent person that you might become. That is the person you would be if you used all of the wisdom that you have available to you, and all of the compassion that you have in your heart, all of the time. It is you without any of the limitations of anger, fear, jealousy, doubt, sadness, vengeance, shame, or resentment. It is what you would be if your life were filled with love and joy.

This is your higher self. Think of it this way. When you first learn to play basketball, you are not as good at it as you can become. The more you practice, the better you get. You make more of your shots. When you get very good, you make most of them. You may never get good enough to make every shot that you try, but you can imagine what that would be like. That image is drawing you toward itself—the image of a player who scores every time she shoots.

Your higher self is like that. It draws you toward itself. It is all that you can become. It is where your life wants you to go. When you communicate with your soul, your higher self is calling to you. This is called the higher-self experience. Your full potential calls you. You feel the possibilities of what you can be, and that helps you become those possibilities.

Some people actually become their higher selves. They live their full potential each moment. They are delighted with Life. They are in awe of Life. They think, speak, and act consciously. They care for Life. They are in communication with their souls continually. You cannot tell where they leave off and their souls begin.

Sometimes this is called enlightenment. Sometimes it is called waking up in your life. It is also called authentic empowerment. It is wanting what your mother ship wants, doing what your mother ship does, speaking what your mother ship speaks, and sailing where your mother ship sails. This is what you were born to do—to become your higher self, to communicate with your mother ship all of the time.

In order to do that, you have to go to a special school.

The Earth School

The Creator gathered all of creation and said, "I want to hide something from the humans until they are ready for it. It is the knowledge that they create their own reality."

"Give it to me," said the salmon. "I will hide it on the bottom of the ocean."

"No," said the Creator. "One day they will go to the bottom of the ocean, and they will find it."

"Give it to me," said the bear. "I will take it into the mountain."

"No," said the Creator. "One day they will dig into the mountains, and they will find it."

"Give it to me," said the eagle. "I will take it to the moon. They will never find it."

"No," said the Creator. "One day they will go to the moon, and they will find it even there."

Then Grandmother Mole rose. Everyone became quiet. They knew that, although she has no physical eyes, Grandmother Mole lives in the breast of Mother Earth and sees with spiritual eyes.

"Put it inside them," she said.

"It is done!" said the Creator.

Now we have discovered the secret. Using multisensory perception requires looking inside yourself. How could you ever find this secret with your five senses? You couldn't. They are designed to look outward. Everything that they detect is outside of you. Even when your body hurts, it hurts because of something outside of you, like some food that you ate, or a hammer that hit your finger. Eating different food, and keeping the hammer away from your fingers, solve the problems.

This is how we have learned to solve problems. The five senses provide information about things that are outside of you. You think about that information, and then act differently—maybe. If you don't, you keep creating the same consequences—like hurting your finger. When you make the connection between the hammer, your finger, and your pain, you change the way you do things.

Now that we are becoming multisensory, we have information about what happens inside us as well as what happens outside. Insights and hunches become part of the picture. If you take into account only what happens outside of you, you are not seeing the whole picture.

Have you ever been to a movie that is so good you forget that you are in the theater? You cry and scream or laugh. The suspense, or the sorrow, is unbearable. You are carried away.

If you were a student of cinema, you would look for things while you watch the movie, like how the story unfolds, which scenes follow which, and what camera angles are used.

The Earth school is a 3-D, full-color, big-screen, multimedia, interactive movie. Getting carried away is easy because it is intimate, exciting, and always changing. If you study this movie—the Earth school—like a student of cinema studies movies, you see that nothing in it is accidental. Everything happens for a reason, just as it does in a theater. This movie is your life. The more you use your intuition, the more you see how it is constructed and what it is telling you.

Each morning a young man jogged past a small house. Each morning, a small black dog charged toward him, barking loudly. It didn't attack him, but it made a lot of noise.

One morning as the dog lurched toward him, barking loudly, the man thought, You spend a lot of energy trying to prove that you are bigger than you are. Why don't you relax and enjoy yourself?

A few steps later, another thought came to him. Am *I* the one who spends a lot of energy trying to prove that I am something I'm not?

That thought changed his life. He is still grateful for it. Now he looks forward to the little dog charging toward him barking.

These kinds of thoughts are multisensory perception. When the young man got angry each morning, he was carried away by the movie. When he realized something about himself that changed his life, he began to see the movie differently. He became a student—a student in the Earth school.

Multisensory perception allows you to study the movie— your life—while you are starring in it. It also allows you to see something else—you are the director of your movie, too. You decide what words to say next. You decide how you will respond to each scene. You make the movie intense or fun, boring or exciting. You play a helpless fool or a wise hero. When you realize that, your life becomes very interesting to you, no matter what is happening.

During World War II the Nazis put a man named Victor Frankl into a concentration camp. They did the worst things that you can imagine to him. They killed people that he loved. They tortured him, and took away everything that he had. He worked in the bitter cold and slept on boards in a frozen barrack. There were so many people on the boards that no one could even roll over! He had just enough food to starve slowly.

How would you like to be in that movie? If you were the director, how would you have Victor finish the scene?

This is how Victor played it. One morning his work party was stumbling down a rocky road in the dark. In the icy wind, while the guards were shouting and hitting them with rifle butts, Victor realized something that changed his life. He realized that his highest goal—the "ultimate goal"— he could reach for was love!

Victor did not become a victim. He did not hate his persecutors and belittle himself. He did not say, "Why me?" or "This is unfair." When you say those things you have no power.

Victor stepped into the greatness of his soul. Instead of making the star—himself—into someone who hates, vows revenge, or collapses in humiliation, he made him a hero who strives to love no matter what. This is one of the best movies that I have heard about. I hope that I can make my movie as good as this one. Do you think you can make yours this good?

Your movie began when you were born and it will end when you die. In between, you play the starring role and direct the action. Your movie doesn't exist apart from the movies of everyone you know and everyone you will ever meet. Each of them is also starring in and directing his or her own movie. You set the stage for them and they do the same for you. That is how the Earth school works.

When you see that you are the director of your movie, you see that you choose everything in it. But what about all of the terrible and painful things that no one would ever choose, like being tortured in a death camp? What about being born with a crooked spine, or abused as a child? How do they get into your movie?

How do they get into anyone's movie?

Reincarnation

"The clouds are Father Sky's gift to Mother Earth," said the old man. Slowly he raised his arms above his gray head, looking toward the sky.

"When the clouds are full," he said, looking directly at me, "they open, and rain falls. When your mother was full, she opened and you fell to the Earth. This is a story about a raindrop, like you.

"This raindrop landed in a meadow. Then it joined other drops and they became a trickle. That trickle became a stream and the stream became a river. Then the river flowed into the ocean.

"The sun smiled on the ocean, and some of the water turned into mist. It rose toward Father Sky, where it became a cloud. When the cloud was full, it opened and another raindrop fell to Mother Earth. It was not the same raindrop, but it came from the same ocean. Then it began its journey back to the ocean, too.

"I heard that story when I was a young boy." He smiled. Then he offered me a cup with some water in it.

"Water is holy," he said as I drank.

We are all made from the same holy stuff, like the clouds, the raindrops, the rivers, and the ocean. The "stuff" that we are made of is Life. Some people call it Consciousness. Some call it Love. Others call it Spirit. Nonphysical Teachers are made of the same holy stuff. You and your soul are made of it, too. The story of you and your soul is like the story of the ocean and the raindrops.

Before television was invented, people listened to the radio together. Some radio adventures took months to tell. Each episode was part of a larger story. For example, the hero gets knocked over a cliff. On the way down, he grabs a root growing out of the rocks. Using all of his strength, he pulls himself onto a narrow ledge. Then he looks up and sees a grizzly bear coming toward him! That is where the episode ends, and the next one begins.

New things happen in each episode, but only some of them get resolved—the hero almost dies, but finally he's OK. Other things don't get resolved. What about the bear? Each episode ends with "To be continued."

Your life is like that. It is the latest episode in a larger story. Your birth was not the beginning of a new story. It continued one that began before you were born. You picked up where the last episode left off. The last episode ended with a death. That is how episodes begin and end in the Earth school—with a birth and a death.

Reincarnation

In the Earth school, the hero talks, acts, and dresses differently in each episode. In one, she is a Mexican mother with eight children. In another, he is a Chinese peasant. In yet another, she is a German nun. It doesn't matter what role the hero plays. Each episode is still part of the same larger story. That is the story of your soul.

In the Earth school, an actor who betrays someone in one episode always plays a person who gets betrayed in another. You always experience what you create. If you don't experience it before you die—before the episode you are in comes to an end—you experience it in another episode—another lifetime. In the East that is called karma. It is also called reincarnation. The two go together.

That is how things that are so painful that you would never choose them get into your movie. They are carryovers from the last movie you made—the last episode in the story of your soul. That movie, like the one you are in now, is part of the story of your soul. Your five senses cannot see that story. They can only see the episode that you are in now.

If you could see all of the movies that you are in, you would look at the life that you are living now very differently.

As we become multisensory, that is exactly what is happening.

A Higher Form
of Reasoning I

"You have not taken a course that is required for your second year," said the dean, frowning across his desk.

Fear tightened Jenifer's stomach.

"How can that be?" she asked. "I've taken everything I was told to take."

"Maybe so," continued the dean, "but you haven't taken a course that you need for next year."

"Can I take it with my second-year courses?" she asked, more nervous now.

"You could," he said, "but this course isn't taught again until next summer. I'm sorry, but you will have to drop out of school until you complete it. You can begin again the semester after you do."

"That will be more than a year!" she exclaimed.

"I understand," said the dean, "but the rules are the rules."

Jenifer tried not to cry when she left the dean's office. All of her energy, money, and focus had gone into becoming a nurse. Her ex-husband didn't think she could do it without him, but she had been admitted to nursing school. She questioned whether she could do it with her young daughter still at home, but she had finished the first year. She had begun a new life for herself, but what could she do now?

She went to her adviser's office.

"Why didn't you tell me about that course?" she asked.

"I made a mistake," he said, upset with himself. "I'm sorry."

Jenifer dropped out of nursing school.

A month later, a speeding car hit her aging father, broke some of his ribs, and changed Jenifer's life forever. Sometimes, when she visited him at the hospital, he recognized her. At other times he did not. Sometimes he saw people by his bed when no one was there. At other times he didn't notice them when they were.

When the hospital could keep him no longer, Jenifer put him in a nursing home. Then they ran out of insurance money, so Jenifer had to sell his house—the same house that she and her daughter called home.

Can you imagine doing all of this at the same time? Taking care of your father, finding a nursing home, selling a house, working two jobs, and taking care of your daughter? Each of these is a very big thing to do. Jenifer did all that and even managed to buy a small house to live in.

By the end of the year, Jenifer had learned to support herself and her daughter, and lived with her in their own house. She returned to school and took the course that she needed when it was taught, and enrolled again in the nursing program. By the time her father passed on, she had become a nurse.

What had seemed unfair to Jenifer at the time—being forced to leave school—now seemed like a blessing. Her adviser's mistake gave her the time she needed to take care of her father, and transform her life in the process. If she had known this when she spoke with the dean, she wouldn't have been upset. She would have seen things very differently.

Have you ever felt that something terrible was happening to you, but later, when you looked back on it, you realized that it was a good thing? That happens to everyone. When you realize that everything that happens to you is for your good, all of the time, you are seeing your life the way your soul sees it.

Even if what happens is painful, like the death of a friend, or being abused, you can still realize—even while it is happening—that it is for your good. If you practice thinking this way, you will save yourself a lot of anger and fear, just as Jenifer could have done.

This is a new way of reasoning. Most people reason the old way. If it hurts, they think, or keeps me from doing what I want, it's not good. Then they get upset, angry, frightened, jealous, and sad. The old way of reasoning always causes these feelings. It makes you feel like a victim—of someone else, or of the Universe. The new way of reasoning makes you feel grateful, the way that Jenifer felt when she looked back on her life.

Which way would you rather feel?

As we become multisensory, the new way of reasoning—which is a much higher way of reasoning than the old way—becomes natural. The five senses told Jenifer that her father had been hurt, but they could not tell her how perfect that was for her, much less for her father. Multisensory perception allows you to see that what happens every moment is perfect, no matter what it is.

Even if you can't see that, you can still know it.

That is using the higher form of reasoning.

A Higher Form
of Reasoning II

"The most important thing of all is to bless everyone all the time."

Around the man's neck was a necklace of fresh flowers. His sandals were simple and well worn.

"Think about what you can bless every time you meet someone. It may be his smile, or gentleness, or intelligence. She may be a mother, or a nurse, or someone who makes people feel good about themselves."

His hair was graying, but his vitality captivated everyone in the room.

"There is always something about everybody that you can find to bless. When you are looking for it, you will find it."

He smiled broadly at his audience.

"Just in case," he continued, "I am going to give you an emergency blessing. You can use it if you can't find one thing about someone to bless."

I had never heard a Hawaiian shaman speak before. I couldn't imagine what he was going to say next.

"Tell yourself," he said solemnly, " 'His exhalation feeds the plants.' "

The whole room burst into laughter.

Outside a gentle breeze stirred palm leaves, and I could hear the ocean below. Hawaii was as beautiful and healing as I had imagined.

I thought about what the kahuna said for a long time. I am still thinking about it. What kind of world would this be if everyone were blessing everyone all the time?

You cannot judge and bless someone at the same time. So when you think that someone is treating you unfairly, or rudely, or trying to hurt you, you will not be able to bless him or her. If you really want to bless everyone you meet, you will need to bless people like this, too.

Here is another emergency blessing that you can use. Say to yourself, "This person is bringing me a lesson that is very important for me to learn. If it were not for this person, I might not be able to learn it."

Just like the kahuna's emergency blessing, this blessing is always true, too.

My first talk in England was in an old church in downtown London. Outside the church, elegant shoppers, people rushing home, and people who didn't have homes crowded the sidewalks. Inside, everything was peaceful and beautiful. Paintings hundreds of years old decorated the ceiling, and all the windows were stained glass.

After the talk, some people gathered around me to ask questions and say hello. We were just beginning to talk when their faces suddenly became very frightened. In the next moment, I felt something hit me on the back of my neck. I spun around and saw, to my surprise, a small, disheveled man. He was glaring at me wildly. He had not hit me hard, but I felt that he had tried to.

Without speaking, he came toward me. I held up my hand in front of me, and he stopped a few inches from it.

"Why are you so angry?" I asked.

He mumbled something, but all I heard was "evil." Abruptly he turned his back to me, walked to the altar, and knelt. I could see that he was praying.

Then he stood up and came toward me again. I didn't want to fight with him, but I didn't want him to hit me again, either. Suddenly I had the idea to look down. When I did, I couldn't see his eyes anymore, but I could see his legs in my peripheral vision. He took a few more steps in my direction, then, without a word, turned and walked quickly out of the church.

A policeman arrived a few minutes later.

"I know this man well," he told me, apologetically. "He is a troublemaker. If you will file charges, I will have him arrested."

Although I was so upset I was shaking, I didn't want to have the man arrested. I knew that he had done what he thought was right, even though I didn't like what he did. I was still touched by the sight of him praying. I also remembered reading that Gandhi told a policeman the same thing after Gandhi was beaten up. I was hardly beaten up, but I felt that I might be feeling what Gandhi did.

When I got back to my apartment, I was still trembling. I closed the door as fast as I could and locked all three of the locks. If there were more, I would have locked them, too. I tried to go to sleep, but I couldn't. I kept thinking about what had happened. Then a completely unexpected thing happened. I realized something that changed my life.

I had not struck back! I, an ex–Green Beret officer, a combat veteran, an ex–motorcycle rider, a mountaineer, had not struck back! I, who had tried for most of my life to be "manly," who was so afraid of being humiliated, who had always struck back, had not struck back!

In that moment, a very big fear in me disappeared. I didn't even know that I had this fear, but I did. It was the fear of not being able to live what I wrote about in *The Seat of the Soul,* which is a book about creating harmony, cooperation, sharing, and reverence for Life, no matter what. I was afraid that I might not be a strong enough, or good enough, person to do that when things got tough. I was even more afraid that others would discover that about me.

I had not struck back! I had not used my fists! I had not even defended myself—at least, not the way I used to. I *could* create harmony. I *could* revere Life! I *could* share and cooperate, even in hard times. I *did* do those things! This was a very big thing for me. I didn't realize until that moment how big my fear was. Suddenly it was gone. I laughed and cried at the same time. I didn't wonder about myself anymore. Something in me had changed, and I felt it. I fell asleep and slept soundly.

The next day I told my host in London what happened.

I thought he might be angry at his countryman for treating me so badly, but instead, he became very thoughtful. Then he said, "You may have given this man a great gift. You know that he starts fights. Since he is little and weak, he probably gets the worst of them. You may have allowed him, for the first time, to leave with his dignity."

Suddenly I began to cry, again. The idea that I might have given this man a gift as big as the one he gave me made me feel very good. I didn't see him as a drunk or a troublemaker anymore. I saw him as a friend. I still do, and I am very grateful for him. How else could I have found the answer to the question that had tormented me for so long? I needed to experience for myself what I would do when I was threatened, and he allowed me to do that. Being attacked from behind was a very unpleasant experience when it happened, but now I am thankful for it. I will always be grateful to the man who attacked me, and bless him. He gave me a lesson that I needed very much to learn, and he did it in the most gentle way that I can imagine.

There is even more to this story.

Glastonbury, a small town south of London, was the real reason I went to England. Have you heard of King Arthur and the Knights of the Round Table? Arthur and his queen, Guinevere, are buried in an ancient abbey in Glastonbury. I was strongly drawn to this place, but I didn't know why. So I went there to find out.

It was a sunny day when I arrived, and it didn't take me long to find the grave. It was marked by a rectangle of small stones on the grass. I was sitting on the ruins of a cathedral wall, looking at the grave, when a group of tourists came by.

One of them stepped on the stones while he was taking a picture.

I was furious with him. How could he be so insensitive? King Arthur was my hero, and a lot of other people's, too. Even if he weren't, his grave shouldn't be walked on like that! I had the urge to charge wildly across the grass, hurl myself through the air, and smash into this man with a flying tackle. I even saw myself doing just that.

In the midst of this violent fantasy, I suddenly realized that I was thinking about doing exactly what the man in the church had done to me! The man in the church thought that I was "evil." He even prayed while he was attacking me. He probably felt as righteous as I did when I thought about tackling the man with the camera. The only difference was that I didn't actually do it.

This was a humbling experience for me. It made me realize how much like my attacker I was. That made me feel very close to him, like a brother. I had seen him as a friend when I left London, but now I felt he was a relative, too. I was grateful for everything that had happened to me, and especially for my new brother.

This is what the kahuna meant when he said to bless everyone all the time. It is also using the higher form of reasoning. When you see that everyone you meet and everything that happens to you brings you lessons that are important for you to learn, you become grateful for everyone and everything.

Then you begin to see your life in a very different way.

A Higher Form of
Reasoning and Justice

"Air Canada Three twelve, this is San Francisco Approach Control. Turn right to two-seven-zero and descend to five thousand feet," said the air-traffic controller.

"Turn right to two-seven-zero degrees, descend to five thousand, Air Canada Three twelve," Jeff repeated to Approach Control.

The atmosphere in the pilots' compartment was tense. It had been a rocky ride from Vancouver, all in instrument flight conditions. They were fifteen minutes late, and the weather was closing in below them.

"Air Canada Three twelve, contact San Francisco tower on one-one-eight-point-six-zero. Good night."

"San Francisco tower, one-one-eight-point-six-zero. Air Canada Three twelve. Good night, sir."

Jeff and his copilot, Carolyn, glanced at each other. She was glad he was with her on the flight deck. His eighteen years of experience had given him a fatherly composure that he sustained through sunny skies and ice storms. It had calmed many copilots. This time, though, Carolyn sensed his concern.

We'll make it, she said to herself. No problem.

Through the mist, a long row of lights appeared below them. Then the runway, outlined in white dots. The huge aircraft touched down as gently as a swan on a calm lake. As Carolyn brought the enormous engines into reverse thrust and Jeff braked, they both sighed in relief.

This had been a tough flight, but in the main cabin there were no sighs of relief, no cries of "Well done!" and no feelings of appreciation. There was no main cabin. Jeff and Carolyn sat, sweating, in a large black box in a hangar, with a team of technicians around it.

Have you ever heard of a flight simulator? Pilots practice in them before they fly a real airplane. Jeff and Carolyn were learning how to fly an airplane that was bigger than any they had flown before.

The instruments in a flight simulator look exactly like the instruments in a real airplane. The control wheel feels exactly like the control wheel in a real airplane, too. Even the views out the windows look the same as they do in a real airplane.

When pilots pull the control wheel in a simulator back, their instruments show a climb. When they look out the windows they see that they are climbing. When they fly into turbulent air they shake like they would in a real airplane, and when they make a rough landing they bounce like they would in a real airplane. Once pilots are inside a flight simulator, they can't tell whether they are in a real airplane or not. They get sweaty in rough weather and feel nervous landing at new airports at night.

A movie theater is a simulator, too. During a movie, you forget that you are sitting in a theater, and that the people you see are moving images on a screen. Even so, you can always look around—if you can remember—and see that you are really in a big, dark room.

Soon you won't have to visit a theater to see a movie. You will be able to put on a helmet that has earphones and a screen built inside it. Then everything that you see and hear, no matter where you look, will be the movie. Even if you look behind you, you will still see the movie. This is called a virtual reality.

Virtual realities don't always begin and end in the same way like movies do. Movies follow a script. They always start the same, play out the same, and end the same. Virtual realities shift from one script to another in a moment. When you make a decision, the virtual reality responds. When you make a different decision, the virtual reality responds in a different way. Whatever you decide causes something to happen.

Can you imagine a virtual reality that uses *all five* of your senses—not just seeing and hearing, but also taste, touch, and smell? You can talk to characters and they talk back. You can touch characters and they touch back. You can even eat, taste the food, and feel full afterward.

How long do you think it will be before you can go to this kind of movie?

A Higher Form of Reasoning and Justice

You are in one now. Every time you make a decision, something happens. When you make a different decision, something different happens. What happens depends on what you decide. Wherever you look, all that your five senses can see is the movie. You can't see outside the theater, but you can decide what the movie is about. You do that with each of your decisions. This is a very important thing to know, because your life is the movie.

Every decision you make causes something to happen. Sometimes it happens right away. Sometimes it takes a while. Either way, you choose. Once you understand this, you can make your movie the way that you want it to be.

To change your movie, you have to make different decisions. That is why some frightened people stay frightened, some angry people stay angry, and so on. They keep making the same decisions. Of course, the decisions that they make always seem different to them because situations change, but when you are angry or frightened in your movie, it doesn't matter what you are frightened or angry about. It only matters that you are frightened or angry. When you stop choosing to be angry or frightened, your movie—your life—becomes less frightening and less angry.

You can always see the choices you are making by looking at your movie. If your life has a lot of angry people in it, you are choosing to be angry. If it has a lot of loving people in it, you are choosing to be loving. This is the way it is for everyone. Each person has his or her own movie, and each person decides what to put in it.

Your movie is your flight simulator. When you are loving and kind, you pull the control wheel back, and it shows a climb into blue skies. Kind and loving people come into your life. When you are angry, jealous, or frightened, you push the control wheel forward, and it shows a dive into dark clouds. Angry, jealous, and frightened people come into your life.

The flight simulator doesn't judge you whether you decide to climb or dive. It always shows you exactly what you are doing.

When you see your life this way, you are learning how to fly.

PART II

How It Works

Emotional Awareness

When I was in the army, I was too afraid to feel how frightened I was. I knew that I was frightened to jump out of airplanes, and to fight with real bullets. That is why I considered myself to be so brave—because I was afraid of these things, but I did them anyway. What I did not know at the time was how afraid of *everything* I was.

If someone had said to me, "You are afraid of everything," I would have become very angry. I saw myself as a brave person, not a frightened one. I did not know how frightened I was to meet new people, to try and fail, to be rejected, and to be incapable of what was expected of me.

I got into arguments. I criticized everyone and everything. I hid my feelings. I did all of these things because I was frightened. I could not stop being frightened until I discovered how frightened I was. I thought I knew what I was feeling, but I didn't.

A woman once thought about adopting a boy in her neighborhood. He was eight years old, and his parents were alcoholics. After a while, she realized that she could not take on the responsibility of adopting him.

When the boy was fifteen, he began using drugs. He became angry and nasty toward everyone, including her. For seven years, she didn't say anything about how she felt. Then she hurt so much that she wrote him a letter. She told him how angry she felt, and how hurt she was. While she was writing the letter, she remembered fondly how he had been when he was younger—so sensitive and tender. She realized in that moment how painful it must have been for him when he found out that she was not going to adopt him. She put that in her letter, too.

A few days later, he called. He was tender and sensitive, just as he used to be. He was crying, too. Underneath all of his anger was a terrible pain—the pain of learning that she would not adopt him. He hadn't realized how much he had been hurting all these years. Being angry kept him from feeling his pain.

I could not stop trying to prove to others how brave I was, because that kept me from feeling how frightened I was. The boy and I both thought we knew what we were feeling, but we didn't. I knew that I was afraid of doing dangerous things, but not that I was afraid of people. The boy knew he was angry, but he didn't know how much he hurt.

Becoming aware of your emotions means more than feeling frightened of some things, and feeling angry at others. It means becoming aware of *everything* that you are feeling. Until you do, there will always be parts of yourself that you don't know about. Some of them are angry. If you don't know about them, you will get angry sometimes, whether you want to or not. Some parts of you are frightened. If you don't know about those parts, you will get frightened sometimes, whether you want to or not.

The parts of yourself that you don't know about are the parts that surprise you. Have you ever decided to make up after an argument, but when you see your friend you start to argue again? You thought you were going to make up, but a part of you was still angry. That part had another idea. It surprised you because you didn't know about it.

Have you ever met someone that you instantly liked, or instantly disliked? That is also what it feels like to have parts of yourself that you don't know about. All of the parts of yourself have their own likes and dislikes. If you don't know about them, you will suddenly find yourself liking or disliking what they do.

Almost everyone has parts of themselves that they don't know about. The strongest parts of yourself that you don't know about are your obsessions, compulsions, and addictions. They are so strong that if you don't know about them, they do whatever they like, no matter what you want. You feel as if you don't have any choice. People who can't stop drinking alcohol are like that. So are people who can't stop using drugs. They are completely in the power of parts of themselves that they don't even know about.

The only way to get to know about the parts of yourself that you don't know about is through your feelings. You have to get to know what you are feeling—*everything* that you are feeling. Each of the different parts of yourself has its own feelings. When you are aware of everything that you are feeling, you can recognize those parts right away.

If the boy knew about the part of himself that hurt so much, he might not have chosen to be angry all the time, but he didn't know about that part, so when it got angry, he got angry. It was almost always angry, and so he was almost always angry, too.

Until you know the angry and frightened parts of yourself, they make the decisions for you. Once you get to know about a part of yourself, it doesn't stop having its feelings and wanting to do the things that it wants to do, but it doesn't surprise you anymore. You don't find yourself getting angry without noticing it, or being angry all the time, sometimes without knowing why. You can decide if you want to act as angry as the angry part of yourself, or as frightened as the frightened part of yourself. You get to choose.

The Buddhists say there are eight winds. They are gain and loss, praise and ridicule, credit and blame, and suffering and joy. If you aren't aware of them, they will blow you away like dry leaves in an autumn breeze. For example, when someone praises you, and that tastes sweet, like candy in your mouth, you are being blown away by the wind of praise.

One day in ancient China a young man thought he had become enlightened. He wrote a poem to his master about how he was not blown by the eight winds. Then he sent it to his master who lived three hundred miles up the Yangtze River.

When his master read the poem, he wrote "Fart, Fart" on the bottom and sent it back.

The more the young man read those words, the more upset he got. At last he decided to visit his master. In those days, a three-hundred-mile trip up the Yangtze River was a very difficult journey.

As soon as he arrived, he went straight to his master's temple. "Why did you write this?" he asked, bowing. "Doesn't this poem show that I am no longer blown about by the eight winds?"

"You say that you are no longer blown by the eight winds," replied the master, "but two little farts blew you all the way up here."

What winds are blowing you?

I could not stop trying to prove how brave I was until I discovered how frightened I was. A lot of winds were blowing me around. The young man could not stop being angry until he discovered how much he hurt. A lot of winds were blowing him around, too. This is what happens when you are not aware of what you are feeling.

When you know what you are feeling, that changes.

A friend of mine in Hawaii was surfing just after a storm. The waves were very big. One of them caught her and held her down for a long time.

"I was terrified," she said. "I couldn't hold my breath any longer, and I didn't know which way was up."

Suddenly she said to herself, "I am in the presence of fear. Now what?" Then she relaxed and the wave carried her back to the beach.

She recognized the wind, and it stopped blowing her.

When that happens, you become able to do something very important.

Responsible Choice

A samurai came to see Hakuin, the Zen master.

"Is there a Heaven and a Hell?" the samurai asked.

"Look at you!" said Hakuin. "You haven't shaved in days. And your clothes are dirty! You call yourself a samurai?"

The samurai grasped the handle of his sword threateningly.

"So!" said Hakuin. "I see you have a sword. It's probably rusty."

At this, the samurai began to draw his sword.

"Here," said Hakuin, "open the gates of Hell."

The samurai grunted, and pushed his sword back into its sheath.

"Here," said Hakuin, "open the gates of Heaven."

Responsible Choice

Making choices is the most powerful thing that you do in your life. Choices liberate and they imprison. They create illness and they create health. They shape your life.

A great American psychologist, William James, had an emotional breakdown over the question "Do I have free will?" Free will means your ability to make choices. Have you ever thought about this? Can you really choose what you will do next, or is your choice always made for you?

William James decided that he did have a choice.

"There is free will!" he declared. "And my first act of free will is to believe in free will!"

That is how William restored his health and regained his strength. His books inspired thousands, including me. That is the power of a choice.

Each choice creates a future. It brings into being one of many possible futures. That is the future that you will live in. For example, you may decide to go to school. Because of that decision, you will meet people that you did not know before. You will influence them, and they will influence you. You will learn new ways of understanding. That future is different from the one you would have brought into being if you decided not to go to school.

Even a choice that seems unimportant, like going to the grocery store or not, creates one future and prevents you from experiencing others. If you go to the grocery store, you might meet someone who will become important to you. If you decide not to go, you might see a television program that changes your life.

You choose your future moment by moment, decision by decision. You do this whether you are aware of it or not.

If you are not aware of it, you create your future unconsciously. That is what happens when you don't know about all of the parts of yourself. The parts of yourself that you don't know about do the choosing. When you are aware of all of the parts of yourself, you do the choosing. Which future would you rather live in—one that you choose, or one that you have not thought about and might not want to happen?

"A dog with short hair and a dog with long hair are always fighting inside me," a man told his friend, "but I am not worried. I know the dog with the short hair will win."

"How do you know?" she asked.

"Because," he replied, "that is the one I feed."

You have dogs fighting inside of you, too. Your anger fights with your patience. Your greed fights with your generosity. If you choose anger, you feed that dog. If you choose patience, that dog grows stronger.

Feeding anger is like joining a club. When you go to that club, you always find angry people. That is what the club is for. It is a place where angry people come together. Whatever you say when you are angry, everyone in the club agrees. Whatever they say when they are angry, you agree. In the exercise room, the lounge, the restaurant—everyone is angry.

Jealousy is another club. You always find jealous people in it. Sorrow is also a club. You always find sad people in it. Joy and gratitude are clubs. They work the same way. You always find happy and grateful people in them.

A tennis club doesn't attract golfers, and a golf club doesn't attract skiers. In the same way, the anger, jealousy, and sadness clubs don't attract joyful or grateful people, and the joy and gratitude clubs don't attract angry, jealous, or sad people.

These clubs are not in different places. Happy and angry people work together in the same buildings. But no matter where they are, angry people are always attracted to other angry people, and happy people are always attracted to other happy people. That is how clubs are formed. If you want to know what clubs you are in, look at the people around you. Are they grateful, angry, happy, or jealous? Are they frightened or generous?

If you like what you see when you look around you, keep doing what you are doing. That will keep you in the same clubs. If you don't like what you see when you look around you, do something different. That is how you join other clubs.

When you see that no club is better than another, you are using the higher form of reasoning.

When you decide for yourself which club to join, that is responsible choice.

Intention

Have you ever wondered what makes an airplane go? The plane is on the runway. The tower tells the pilot, "Cleared for takeoff," and she pushes the throttle forward. The engines roar, and the plane moves.

Why?

You are stopped at a red light. It turns green. You step on the gas pedal, and your car moves.

Why?

When the pilot opens the throttle, part of the roar you hear is the sound of huge blades spinning, like giant fans. They push air backward, and the plane moves forward. Isaac Newton didn't know about jets, but three hundred years ago he discovered that when something pushes against something else, the thing that gets pushed pushes back. The harder it is pushed, the harder it pushes back.

Intention

Jet engines push air. If you don't think so, try standing behind one. The air pushes back. If a fan could push air hard enough, it would blow itself across the room. That is what jet engines do—push air so hard that when the air pushes back, the plane moves down the runway.

The tires on your car push against the Earth. The Earth pushes back. The harder they push, the harder the Earth pushes back and the faster your car goes. When you walk, your feet push against the Earth and the Earth pushes back. You move forward.

For every action there is an equal and opposite reaction. Newton called this the third law of motion. Pushing the air or the ground is the action. Moving forward is the reaction.

Your intentions are your engines. They get you from one place to another. You may think that airplanes fly you from place to place, but actually it is your intentions. Airplanes take off every day, but unless you are on one, you won't go anywhere.

An intention is not a wish. A wish does not cause anything to happen. An intention does. An intention pushes against the way things are in your life. Those things push back exactly the same way. (Remember, for every action there is an equal and opposite reaction.) You can see what your intentions are by looking at what is happening around you. Are the people in your life kind and loving? If so, your intentions are kind and loving. (And you are a member of the love and kindness clubs.) Are the people around you angry or jealous? If so, your intentions are angry or jealous. (And you are a member of the anger and jealousy clubs.)

Your intentions create everything that you experience. For example, if you play baseball, your intentions, not the game, determine what you experience. If you intend to win, you will be anxious before each game. You will be miserable if you lose. You will worry about your teammates, and how they play. If you intend to do your best, your experience will be very different. You will look forward to playing. You will be relaxed and ready for anything. You will be grateful to the other team for giving you the chance to do your best.

Billions of tiny organisms called microbes live on your body. Imagine that they organize themselves into groups and build cities. They don't know that you are alive. They take whatever they need, without asking you or thinking about you. Soon, you are covered with microbes like these, and all of them take anything they want, whenever they want it.

Eventually, you get sick. The microbes notice this because their air gets dirty, their water gets polluted, and their forests start to die.

"We are in trouble," they say to each other. They get so frightened that they organize into environmental movements.

What would you feel like, having billions of frightened microbes on you, each taking what it needs for itself? Does the idea make you feel good, or does it make you itch all over?

Now suppose the microbes that are living on you know that you are alive. They are very grateful for you because everything that they have and everything that they need comes from you. They love you, and they are thinking about good things to do for you all the time.

Which kind of microbes would you want to have growing on you?

Intention

The first kind thinks about itself. Even when it tries to take care of you, it is really only taking care of you in order to take care of itself. The second kind loves you. It takes care of you because it is grateful for you, and happy that you are its home.

People who call the Earth a "resource" are like the first kind of microbe. They want clean air because they want to continue to breathe. People who see the Earth is a wonderful, living Mother are like the second kind. They want the Earth to be healthy because they love her.

Which group are you in?

Actions are like bottles. Your intentions are what you put in the bottles. You can put tea, orange juice, or sour milk in them. You can put grape juice, apple juice, or paint remover in them. What you taste when you drink from them depends on what you put in them.

If you put selfishness into your bottles, that is what comes out when you drink. Selfish people will be around you wherever you go. If you put care for others into your bottles, that is what will come out. Everywhere you go, people will care about you.

If you put the intentions of your soul into your bottles, they are what will come out.

Your soul has four intentions.

Harmony

"My Brother," I said, gathering my courage, "I have an issue with you."

The circle fell silent. No one expected this on the last night of our retreat.

"I do not know whether this issue has to do with you, or only with me. But it is creating a distance in my heart between us."

A restless shuffling of feet and an air of anxiety filled the tent.

"You are too important to me for this to happen, and so I am going to share my issue with you."

As I began to speak, one man, a retired executive, shifted his weight back and forth in his chair. Another put his shoes on as if to leave, then took them off, and then put them back on again. My copresenter, whom I was address-ing, looked at me silently with the quietness of a Buddha.

"I have been told . . ." I started slowly, remembering my intentions. Before I could complete more than a few sen-tences, one of the women in the circle got up and left. A few seconds later, another followed her. The moment I finished, my best friend, who had come from London, shot to his feet.

"Gary!" he shouted angrily, "you have gone too far!"

He had more to say, but before he could finish, Linda's best friend jumped to her feet, too, and joined him.

"I agree!" She glared righteously at me. "He," she said, pointing to my copresenter, "is the only reason I have got-ten anything from this retreat."

"Wow," another woman marveled. "This is the first event I've been to where people are real!"

Then everyone began to speak at once. Some liked what I had to say. Others didn't. Some were angry. Some were frightened. Everyone had an opinion. The hurricane had struck.

My first experiment with creating harmony had begun.

Have you ever felt that there is something that you have to say, no matter what, but you are afraid of saying it? That is what happened to me. Throughout the week, people had come to me with things they wanted to tell me about other people at the retreat.

"If it is important," I told them, "bring it to the family— share it in the circle. If it is not important, let's not talk about it."

Now I had something that was important to me. I had an issue with my copresenter.

This was the first retreat that Linda Francis, my spiritual partner, and I had ever given. I wanted it to end beautifully. I wanted everyone to like me, and to go home with warm memories. How could I confront my copresenter—of all people—on our last night together? Yet how could I ignore the directions that I had given the family throughout the week? These were more than directions. They were at the heart of what makes a real family—saying what needs to be said, even when you are afraid to say it.

Linda and I had decided to dedicate our retreat to exploring authentic power—the alignment of the personality with the soul. On the very first morning, I realized that I must not try to explain authentic power, or even speak about it. We must all live it. My planning went out the window—what I was going to say and when I was going to say it. All that was left were my feelings, minute by minute, about what to do next. I had nothing else to guide me, so I followed them continually. Now the time had come to see where they were leading. I was frightened, to say the least.

I had always been told, "If you don't have something nice to say about someone, don't say anything at all." What I had to say wasn't nice, but I didn't know if it was even about my copresenter. It was something that was bothering me, and the more it bothered me, the more distant I felt from him. How could I know if it were true or not if I didn't ask him about it? But if I kept my questions a secret from the family, I wouldn't be treating them like a real family.

I could not bear the thought of losing the precious moment of our last circle to say what was so strongly in my heart. If I didn't, I knew that I would live with the knowledge that I had something that I needed to say, but I didn't say it. If I did, I might tear our retreat apart, and everyone would go home feeling bad. Have you ever felt that way about your family, or friends? Should you leave things alone, even though everyone can feel that something is not right, or should you talk about it?

I decided to talk about it, but in a different way than I had ever talked about difficult things before. First, I decided exactly why I was going to talk to my copresenter. Was it because I was angry? Was it because I wanted everyone to know that he had done something wrong (if, in fact, he had)? No. It was because I missed feeling close to him. That was my intention—to become close with him again. I promised myself to remember that every moment.

Second, I decided to feel everything inside me, every time I spoke. I used to spend a lot of time thinking, and less time feeling. When I spoke about what I thought, sometimes my mind wandered. I didn't want that to happen. I knew that if I focused on what I was feeling, I would always be present. That is exactly where I wanted to be.

I made another promise to myself, too—to let anything happen. Of course, I wanted to reconnect with my friend, but if he was angry, and I tried to make him feel something else, I wouldn't be respecting him. I wanted our retreat to end happily, but if the people in it became upset, I made up my mind to accept that, also. I decided that my job was to have a clear intention, speak from my heart, and not be attached to the result. The rest was up to my friend and our family.

When the storm struck, it was more violent than I had imagined. Everyone was talking. Some were approving and some were disapproving. Words were flying everywhere. I was surprised at how calm I felt. I had done what I needed to do, and now the matter was where it needed to be—in the hands of the family.

"One of us is outside hurting!" shouted one of the men, louder than the rest. "You two are responsible," he said, pointing to my copresenter and me. "It's your responsibility to find her and bring her back."

Usually, I do not interfere with other people's decisions, but the family now demanded that we look for the young woman who had left, and her friend who had followed. So my copresenter and I left the tent and went out into the warm summer night.

As we walked, we talked. I welcomed the chance to hear him. Until then, he had not had an opportunity to speak. He asked me questions, and I explained my issues again. At last, I asked him, "Do these have anything to do with you?" He thought for a moment, and then said, "No."

"That is what I need to know," I told him, with a feeling of having solved a mystery. "It has only to do with me."

We hugged, but it wasn't a real hug, the kind that makes me feel good. As we walked back, a part of our conversation kept returning to me. In the midst of our talk, he had asked, "Do you feel any jealousy?" "No," I replied, but now I knew this was not true. I was ashamed to admit it, but I felt jealous of my friend. I stopped on the path, and told him so.

To my surprise, he began to cry. Then he began to sob.

"When I was a boy," he said, "I always knew when something was wrong between my father and me. If I asked him, he always said, 'Nothing is wrong,' but I knew something was. All I ever wanted was to be a good boy!" he said through his tears. "You don't know what is being healed in me."

The tenderness of this powerful, intelligent man touched me deeply. I thought of the woman who had left the tent—the one we had come to find. I thought about how much more sensitive I could have been to her. This made me sad, and I began to cry, also.

My tears prompted my copresenter into yet another deep, tender insight, and he began to cry even more. His new crying caused me to see something else about myself, and I began to cry again, too. We had a meltdown. As more and more insights flooded me, I cried until I felt too weak to stand, and he did, too.

At last, I noticed there were still lights in the tent. "I wonder if they are still there?" I whispered.

"Let's see," he replied, and we walked toward the tent, hand in hand.

I was completely unprepared for what we found. Everyone was there, sitting in a circle. The atmosphere was calm and relaxed. People spoke like old friends.

"Would you like to join our circle?" asked one of them.

"Yes!" I exclaimed with relief.

They all laughed, and rearranged themselves to make room. They wanted to see us hug, which was easy because that is what we had just been doing. It was late, and everyone was tired but happy. We stood, held hands, and then all of us went to bed.

The next morning, our last together, was the most beautiful that I can remember. We laughed, cried, hugged, sang, and talked. We cared about each other, and showed it. We were tender, and we were direct. Everyone was included.

The young woman who had left the tent was there, and so was her friend. They had spent the evening sitting quietly by the stream, and now were with us again.

What had happened to transform this angry, shouting group of people into heartfelt friends? What had created this magical intimacy?

This is the story that they told me:

When my copresenter and I left the tent, the turbulence increased. Groups formed for and against me, and for and against my copresenter. Another group formed that didn't approve of either of us. Everyone was angry and opinionated.

Finally, Linda suggested that they all sit in a circle and meditate quietly, whatever that meant to them. After a while, my friend from London, the same one who had criticized me so harshly, rose.

"I am learning something from this," he said. "I want to tell you what I am learning, and I suggest that we go around the circle and everyone share what he or she is learning."

That is what they did. They shared their angers and their fears. They shared their surprise and their excitement. They shared their histories and their aspirations. They spoke from depths they had not reached with each other before. When they had finished, they were a family. Not a play family, but a *real* family. They cared deeply about each other. They spoke directly to one another without fear. They laughed effortlessly, and they cried effortlessly. I felt safe with them, and they felt safe with me and each other.

This was my first experience of harmony. It replaced every idea of harmony that I had. I knew that I wanted to live the rest of my life this way. I was in love with this family, and it was in love with me. The hardest part of our retreat was leaving it. Today, years later, many of us are working together, and many more of us are still in touch.

Now Linda and I experiment with powerful processes like this all of the time. Usually it creates the same wonderful experience. Some people call it community. Others call it family. Everyone agrees that the heart of it is a harmony that is so natural, so satisfying, and so welcomed that life without it—once you have tasted it—is hard to imagine.

I am grateful for this experience because, among other things, it taught me that sometimes it takes a lot of courage to create harmony. It was not easy for me to confront my copresenter on the last night of our retreat. It was not easy for anyone to be there, to share what they needed to share, and listen while others did that, too. Everyone was uncomfortable, but the more willing we were to be uncomfortable with each other, the stronger our bond was afterward.

I saw something else, too. Doing what other people expect you to do *never* creates harmony. To create harmony, you have to come closer to people. Doing what you think will please them moves you farther away. How can you be close to someone when you don't feel that you can be who you are around him or her? Harmony comes from sharing who you are, letting others share who they are, and learning how to do that together.

When everyone thinks the same way, and wants the same things, this is easy. But what about those times when you are with people who want what you do not, or think differently than you? Do you want to create harmony with them?

Your soul does.

Cooperation

We had spoken for several minutes before the voice on the phone said, "You don't know who I am, do you?"

"No," I admitted, though the name sounded familiar.

"I am on television," she said. "I have a talk show called *Oprah*."

I didn't watch television. I lived a reclusive life in the mountains, close to nature, but not too close to people. I was frightened that she might be inviting me to come on her show, but she wasn't. She only wanted to thank me for *The Seat of the Soul*, and to get acquainted. I was touched that my book meant so much to her.

I loved sharing the things in *The Seat of the Soul*, but the idea of sharing on television was overwhelming to me. I never thought that I could cocreate with a friend, talk about things I like the most, and have a good time all at once. I needed to journey further down my path to think about that, and perhaps Oprah needed to journey further down hers.

We stayed in touch over the years, speaking on the phone now and then. Seven years after our first talk, Oprah called again.

"I am restructuring my show this fall," she said. "Will you help me get some clarity?"

I felt a growing excitement.

"I could retire and count the shoes in my closet," she continued, "but I want to *give* something to the world. I want to create television that helps people change their lives."

Suddenly I was electrified. Her words thrilled me.

"I am creating a short segment called 'Remembering the Spirit' at the end of each show. What do you think?"

I thought it was a good idea. When we hung up, I started writing my thoughts. I sent them to Oprah, and a few weeks later a producer called.

"May we send a crew to your house next week?" he asked. "We are taping 'Remembering the Spirit' segments. Yesterday we taped a scholar feeding his chickens. The day before, we taped a woman meditating."

I called Oprah to decline.

"A video of me walking on a mountain will not inspire anyone," I told her.

"No!" she shouted. "Talk about *The Seat of the Soul*! That's what you talk about! Talk about the things in your book."

I felt the electricity again.

"I'll do it!" I exclaimed.

I expected a film crew to come the next week, but another call came instead.

"Will you fly to Chicago tomorrow," asked the producer, "and tape an interview with Oprah the next day?"

This time I felt very different than I had during my first conversation with Oprah. This time, her invitation felt exactly right. I didn't feel frightened. I didn't feel overwhelmed. I felt like a surfer feels when a perfect wave comes. All I needed to do was to stand up on my board. I knew the ride would be wonderful.

Linda felt the same way, and we flew to Chicago to meet Oprah.

It was fun. Oprah became part of our family immediately. She thought I might look like a mountain man, and have a big stomach and a gray beard.

"He looks normal!" she exclaimed. "I can put him on television!"

We prayed together that our show would be the most empowering we could make it. Then we sat down in front of the cameras to talk. Oprah planned to tape another show after our interview, but it was canceled. We talked for two and a half hours! When we were done, she said excitedly, "I can make several 'Remembering the Spirit' segments from this!"

Then she thought of somethine else.

"I'll make a Christmas Special from this interview—and give it to my viewers as a holiday gift!"

She did. It aired Christmas Eve afternoon.

Our time together was that easy. I had met a new friend.

Cooperation

We had talked about things that I love the most. We decided to do it again, and Linda and I went home.

The results were as spectacular as they were easy. Oprah made eight "Remembering the Spirit" segments from our interview. *The Seat of the Soul* appeared on the *New York Times* Bestseller List. By the time the Christmas Special aired, it was already number one.

Cooperation feels like that—it is as easy as play. It isn't just working together on a common goal, like making money, electing a president, or raising a family. That is the joint pursuit of external power. When people do that, their goal is the most important thing to them. When they reach it, they find other goals in common, or they go different ways.

From the point of view of your soul, cooperation is play. People cooperate because they *want to be together*, not because they share goals. People come first, and goals come second. People who want to be together always think of things to do together, just as children always think of games to play.

Who do you want to play with?

Sharing

I went to high school in a small town in Kansas. The best thing about it for me was my debate coach, Dan. Dan also taught English and, occasionally, drama. I was glad that he wasn't my English teacher because his English was horrible. I cringed every time he said things like, "He don't . . ." but after a while, I didn't care how Dan spoke. Knowing him changed my life, and I still love him.

Our tiny school competed in debate against huge schools in Kansas City, and medium-sized schools around the state. We usually won the state championship, and everything else. The walls of our classroom were covered with shelves full of trophies. So were the walls of the hall outside, down to the next classroom.

We traveled in a military surplus van, which had been

painted blue. We called it the Blue Bomb, and made bets about where it would break down next. I was too young to know how uncomfortable the Blue Bomb was, but, years later, I realized that Dan was not. He drove us everywhere, to tournament after tournament, weekend after weekend. I looked forward to debate class. We met at Dan's house in the evenings to practice in the basement. His daughters grew up sharing their house with debaters.

I am not the only one whose life was changed by Dan. I soaked up his warmth, humor, and optimism, and so did everyone else. He was the teacher and we were the students, but there was a bond between us that felt like friendship to me. I believe now that it was. He took the time from his evenings and weekends, from his family, and from his love for golf to be with us. He gave freely of himself, and, without really knowing much about debate, we won tournament after tournament, like the classes before us and the classes after.

When I applied to Harvard, Dan wrote a long, passionate letter of recommendation for me. Someone must have spell-checked his English. I believe his letter was why I was accepted. Dan passed on long ago. I am now older than he was when he drove me to tournaments, but he is still a part of me.

That is because Dan knew how to share.

Sharing doesn't mean simply letting a friend drive your car, lending some money, or even helping a neighbor in need. It means giving something of yourself that is important.

After running for a year, Linda realized that she wanted to run a marathon. She and her running partner, Terry, decided to train together and run one together in the fall. They intensified their schedule, running six miles a day every day, and ten miles once a week. As the day of the marathon approached, they were both healthy and ready. The race started well, and went that way until mile twenty, when Terry's leg began to hurt. His pace dropped off, and then he slowed to a walk. As he did, Linda slowed also, and at last began to walk with him.

"Go on," he told her. "I'm not going to finish."

"Well, why don't you go just a little farther?" she suggested.

He did, but a little while later, he said the same thing. "Go on. I'm not going to make it."

"Let's go just a little farther," she suggested again, and again he did.

They both finished the race that way—walking, with Terry going just a little farther time after time.

"Didn't you want to finish the race running?" I asked her later.

"Of course I did," she said, "but I knew how Terry would feel if he didn't finish."

That is sharing.

When you give something as important as that, you also receive a gift. Once I was invited to a lomi lomi class. Lomi lomi is an ancient Hawaiian form of body work and lifestyle. One of the students there was wearing a beautiful carved hook around his neck. It was more than jewelry. It was powerful and graceful. I felt soothed and calmed when I looked at it. When the class was over, he came toward me. A painful expression crossed his face, and he took the hook from his neck and put it around mine.

"This is for you," he said, towering above me. "In Hawaii, we use hooks like these to catch what we need."

I was thrilled. I decided to use my hook to catch patience

and wisdom. I wore it every day. I put it on in the morning, and slept with it by my bed.

Several years later, a group of us were standing on Mount Shasta, a holy mountain in California. We prayed in a circle, and gave thanks for the retreat we had just given together. One of us, Benjamin, offered to sing a song that he heard in a dream. As he knelt on the Earth, preparing to sing, something surprising happened to me. I wanted to give Benjamin my hook!

I remembered the painful expression on the face of the young Hawaiian who gave the hook to me. Just as he had done, I took the hook from my neck. Then I put it around Benjamin's.

Giving Benjamin my hook showed me how much I had changed. Before, I could not have given away something so precious to me. Now I couldn't not give it to Benjamin. The gift that I received was seeing how much I had changed, and what a considerate person I had become. Even if Benjamin hadn't liked my hook—even if he had thrown it away—the gift that I got from giving it would be mine forever.

When I saw Benjamin next, years later, he was still wearing his hook. It means a lot to him. That is why I suspect that, sooner or later, he will give it away.

If you give only what is easy to give, you can't grow. That is like giving away tomatoes when your garden is full of tomatoes. Sharing things that are important is like giving away tomatoes when you only have a few left—and you love tomatoes. You have to care about people to do that.

This is the kind of sharing your soul wants to do.

Reverence
for Life

The car in front of me was still at the stop sign. His left-turn signal was still blinking. One car after another passed through the intersection, with lots of room between each of them.

"What is he waiting for?" I asked impatiently.

At last the car moved. I followed it through the intersection and, a moment later, found myself behind it again. The driver was not in a hurry. There were no cars in front of him, but he was going very slowly.

I was late for my appointment.

"He must be senile," I fumed.

The road widened, and I passed as soon as I could. When I did, I looked over to see the driver. It was Herb, my friend!

I was delighted to see him. A moment earlier I was furious with him. Now I was happy to see him. I waved and he waved back.

Everything had changed because I saw something that I hadn't seen before—the driver was my friend.

Reverence is like that. It is seeing something that you haven't seen before. You recognize friends wherever you look.

The lean man closed the door to his old truck. It was stacked high with firewood for me. Slowly he walked toward me, and put out his hand.

"Good day," he said. "Your firewood will cost more this year."

I didn't expect that news. I didn't like it, either, but there was nothing I could do. Winter was coming, and I had waited too long to buy my wood.

"Stack it there," I told him, pointing to the empty woodshed.

"My nephew will do that," he said, nodding to the boy in his truck. "I'll be back with the rest."

I felt angry.

The boy began to stack the wood. I noticed how carefully he placed each piece.

"Do you like working for your uncle?" I asked, making some conversation while I watched him work.

"Yes," he said, without stopping.

"Why?" I asked.

"This will pay for my school clothes," he said, pointing to the unstacked pile of wood he had thrown from the truck. Then he smiled directly at me.

"We don't have any money."

I melted. Suddenly, I liked being with him, and I liked his uncle, too. I wasn't angry anymore. I was glad to buy the boy's clothes for school. It seemed to me that we had a perfect arrangement. I get firewood, and they get school clothes.

I saw something that I hadn't seen. Before, I saw people selling wood. Afterward, I saw an uncle and his nephew working to buy school clothes.

Reverence is like this, too. It is seeing beneath the surface. Before I recognized Herb, I saw only a slow driver. Afterward, I still saw a slow driver, but I also saw my friend. Before I talked with the boy, I saw only a woodcutter and his nephew. Afterward, I still saw a woodcutter and his nephew, but I also saw two friends.

Your soul always sees friends. That is because it sees beneath the surface. When you see a friend wearing a beautiful dress, do you think she is beautiful because of her dress? When you see her in a dress that you don't like, isn't she still your beautiful friend? When you see with reverence, you see everyone as a beautiful friend, even if he is driving slowly, like Herb, or doing something you might not like, such as raising the price of your firewood.

When you see with reverence, you see holiness in everything. Holiness is like the friend inside the dress. You see the dress, and you see your friend, too. Your friend is the important thing, not her dress.

Holiness is like the ocean. What you see with your five senses is like the waves in the ocean. There are so many that you can never see them all. Some are large and some are small. All of them have a different shape, and a different way of moving. All of them change in their own way, and disappear into the ocean in their own way. Each one is unique.

Reverence is loving the ocean.

Authentic Power

"There is a meeting this Friday at the Lawrence Berkeley Laboratory," a friend of mine, a physicist, called one day to say. "It's about quantum physics. Want to come?"

I went out of curiosity. I didn't expect to understand what I heard, but I did. It was the most profound discussion I could imagine, about questions such as "Does consciousness create reality?"

I left the meeting very excited, although I couldn't explain what was exciting me. My friends knew that I was excited, and that it had to do with quantum physics. That was all I knew, too.

I went to the next meeting, and the next. Then I started going every week. I asked questions. I also started reading about quantum physics. Little by little, I began to understand it, and the more I understood, the more excited I became.

I decided to write a book. I wanted to leave a gift for people who would become interested in quantum physics in the future. I asked the physicists at the meeting to help me, and they agreed. My journey had begun.

I had never written a book before, or studied science. That didn't matter to me. I looked forward to reading about physics and writing about physics. I looked forward to talking about physics and thinking about physics. I thought of questions, and tried to answer them.

I had found the most engaging activity of my life. It was also the most fulfilling. When I wrote, I forgot about paying the rent, although I didn't know where I would get the money. I forgot to be angry, which I usually was. I also forgot to be resentful and jealous.

Can you imagine the most beautiful island in the world? At every opportunity, you row to the island. At last your friends tell you, "Don't work so hard. You don't need to row every day to that island. It will still be there tomorrow." That is what my friends told me, but the island was my book, and I never wanted to leave it.

This was my first experience of authentic power.

Authentic power feels good. It is doing what you are supposed to be doing. It is fulfilling. Your life is filled with meaning and purpose. You have no doubts. You have no fears. You are happy to be alive. You have a reason to be alive. Everything you do is joyful. Everything is exciting. You look forward to each day and each night.

You are not worried about doing something wrong, making a mistake, or failing. You do not compare yourself with others. You do not compare what you do with what others do.

You can experience authentic power caring for a child, or cooking a meal. You can experience it building a house, or, like me, writing a book. It doesn't comes from what you are doing. It comes from how you are doing it. You can experience authentic power at work, at school, or anywhere else.

Authentic power is different from external power. External power is the ability to manipulate and control. External power feels different from authentic power. It is trying to impress people, do the right thing, or succeed. It is trying to be better, smarter, stronger, or more beautiful.

The governor of Kyoto arrived at the monastery.

"Give this card to the abbot," he told the monk at the gate. "I have an appointment with him at three o'clock."

When the abbot read the card he said, "I don't know this man. Send him away!"

The monk returned the card to the governor. The governor looked at it, and then crossed out the words *Governor of Kyoto.*

"Give this to the abbot," he said again.

"Show this man in," said the abbot. "I have an appointment with him at three o'clock."

The governor thought that his title would impress the abbot, but the abbot was not impressed. Do you use titles to impress people—like "beautiful," "educated," "strong," and "wealthy"? That is using external power. It is very different from authentic power. You forget to be frightened when you experience authentic power. You are always frightened when you use external power.

External power comes and goes, like the value of your stock portfolio or the number of trees in your orchard. Pursuing it is a full-time job. It is hard to be more beautiful, wealthy, loving, intelligent, kind, or efficient than other people. Sooner or later, someone will be more beautiful, wealthy, loving, intelligent, kind, or efficient than you. Then they will have the external power.

Creating authentic power is a full-time job, too, but it doesn't depend on what happens outside of you.

It depends on what happens inside.

Creating Authentic Power

"There are many types of bread," Tony said with a flourish of his index finger, giving it a little spin and pointing it upward. "Today we will learn how to bake the most basic kind, but, of course, bake it to perfection." He stood behind his counter in the studio. Cameras moved in and out to catch his every motion and smile.

"There is only one way to bake bread," he continued with a grin. "First, you must want to do it. Second, you must have flour, water, yeast, and salt."

So began another of Tony's delightful cooking courses. Across the city, novice and expert cooks alike took notes, or stood in their own kitchens, following Tony step by step.

"First, mix the yeast, flour, and water, like this." He

demonstrated, roughly measuring each ingredient and stirring it in with a wooden spoon. "Then put the dough on a countertop, like this, and begin sprinkling in more flour. Knead the dough as you do, using your hands and arms as well as your fingers, like this." His body rocked rhythmically back and forth as he lovingly kneaded the lump of dough, which was growing softer and more malleable.

"Don't forget to add a little salt, and maybe a little sugar," he continued. "So much of baking is personal taste. Experiment. Let yourself be guided. It's your bread you're baking."

Creating authentic power is like baking bread. First, you have to want to do it. Then you need to follow the recipe. If you do these things, you'll have lots of opportunities to experiment and be guided by your inner promptings. As with bread, it's your own loaf that you are baking. Unlike bread, no one else can bake it for you.

The recipe for authentic power is as simple as the recipe for bread—harmony, cooperation, sharing, and reverence for Life. Those are the ingredients. How you put them together depends upon you, but without all of them, authentic power is not possible any more than bread is possible without the ingredients that are required to make it.

This is how to do it. First, clear the countertop of everything but what you will need to bake authentic power. That means put every intention aside for the moment except the intentions to create harmony, cooperation, sharing, and reverence for Life in your own life.

Second, keep doing it.

Soon you will start to create some harmony, cooperation, sharing, and reverence for Life. The bread is baking. Eventually, you will create these things moment by moment, choice by choice. That is authentic power. Experiences of fulfillment, meaning, and awareness can be created. This is big news.

It is not necessary to be filled with anger, jealousy, sorrow, and fear. All it takes is the desire to create authentic power, and the will to do it—the desire to create harmony, cooperation, sharing, and reverence for Life, and the will to create them when you are angry, jealous, sad, and frightened. Understanding how to create authentic power is easy compared to actually doing it, but the same is true about anything that develops you.

Baseball is easy to understand. Becoming a good player is more difficult. First, you have to get into good condition, and you have to stay that way. Then you have to learn skills, such as pitching, catching, and batting. Then you need to practice, practice, and practice. This requires other people. You need a team to play on, and other teams for your team to play.

Anyone can understand baseball in an afternoon, but no one can become a good player overnight. Everyone needs time to learn, practice, apply, and then learn, practice, and apply again. This takes time and intention. It takes focus and determination.

So does creating authentic power. Knowing how is easy. Just set the intentions to create harmony, cooperation, sharing, and reverence for Life no matter what, and keep them. The rest is learning what these things mean, how to do them, and practice. That takes time. You also need other people to practice with. In this case, you don't have to recruit them. They are always there. They are the ones you get angry at, jealous of, sad about, or frightened of.

To improve your ball game, you have to become aware of yourself. For example, you need to become conscious of how your body moves when you swing the bat. Great batters know exactly what they are doing as they do it. They don't close their eyes and swing. They are conscious of every muscle.

Are you aware of your intentions? When you are angry, what are your intentions? When you are jealous, what are your intentions? Trying to change your intentions when you don't know what they are is like trying to go to New York when you don't know where you are starting from. Going to New York from San Francisco is one thing. Getting there from Paris is another.

When you are aware of all of your intentions, you are like a great batter who is conscious of every muscle as he moves his body toward the ball. He can change what needs to be changed. He knows how to get where he wants to go, because he knows exactly where he is.

When you choose your intentions according to what you want to create, that is responsible choice. When you intend to create harmony, cooperation, sharing, and reverence for Life, your intentions and the intentions of your soul are the same. When that happens, you become authentically powerful.

Creating authentic power is a process. Each time you choose harmony, cooperation, sharing, or reverence for Life, you challenge parts of yourself that want other things.

They are the parts of you that are angry, sad, jealous, and frightened. The more you challenge them, the less power they have over you, and the more power you have over them. Eventually, their power over you disappears.

That is how authentic power is created—intention by intention, choice by choice. You cannot wish it, pray it, or meditate it into being any more than you can wish, pray, or meditate yourself into being a great baseball player. If you want to bake bread, you have to know how to do it. If you want to create authentic power, you have to know how to do that, too.

Then you have to do it.

Forgiveness

"Kill him!" said the brother. His face was set like stone. "Kill him!" said the mother, through her tears. "Kill him!" said the sister, her voice quivering.

Around the council fire each member of the family spoke. In the balance lay the life of the young man sitting restlessly outside. Murder is a terrible thing. Murder of a friend is more terrible yet. Yet there he sat, the blood of his friend still on his hands, awaiting his fate.

"Let us think this through," spoke the grandfather softly. Sorrow deepened the lines on his wrinkled face. Generations spoke through him. "Will killing him return our boy to us?"

"No." "No." "No." The word moved slowly around the

tortured circle, sometimes whispered, sometimes murmured, sometimes spoken spitefully.

"Will killing him help feed our people?" asked the old man, his eyes steady.

Again, "No," then "No," then "No," moved around the circle.

"My brother speaks the truth," said the great-uncle. All faces turned toward him. A tear ran slowly down his cheek. "Let us look at this matter carefully."

They did look at it carefully. They deliberated through the night. Then they called the young man to his fate.

"See that tepee?" they said, pointing to the tepee of the young man he had killed. He nodded. "It is yours now."

"See those horses?" they said, pointing to the dead man's horses. He nodded again.

"They are yours now. You are now our son. You will take the place of the one you have killed."

He looked up slowly to the faces surrounding him. His new life had begun, and so had theirs.

Brown Bear looked across the table at me.

"That happened in the late eighteen hundreds," he said. "They could have killed him. Tribal law gave them the right."

I sat amazed as Brown Bear's words sank into me. Could the family of a murdered boy adopt the murderer as their son?

"The young man became a devoted son," Brown Bear continued. "By the time he died, he was known in all the tribes as the model of a loving son."

This is forgiveness. Authentically empowered people forgive naturally. They forgive because they do not want to carry the burden of not forgiving like heavy suitcases through a crowded airport. The family of the murdered boy could have killed his killer. Instead they took him as their son. That changed their lives and his. They did not know how their decision would affect the young man, but they felt the effects of it on themselves.

They did not have to hate him. They did not have to live with his death in their hearts, as well as the death of their son. Have you ever thought that someone treated you badly, and then thought about it again and again? How did that make you feel? Were you angry, or sad, or frightened? That is what they gave up. Until you forgive, you cannot use all of your creativity. Part of you is thinking about what you have not forgiven. Do you want to live your life that way? Is it worth it? Is anything worth that?

Forgiveness and harmony go together. When you forgive someone, nothing stands between you and that person. Even if the person you forgive does not like you, you have laid your suitcases down. You travel lightly.

When you are harmonious you are playful. You delight in people. Not forgiving stops this. Forgiving opens the door to it.

Harmony does not only mean harmony with other people. Are you in harmony with yourself? Do parts of yourself frighten you, or make you angry? Can you forgive those parts? Are you afraid of dropping the ball, losing the deal, or failing the test? Imagine that each time you get angry at yourself, you put a brick into a backpack that you are wearing. Can you enjoy yourself while you are wearing a backpack full of bricks?

Are you in harmony with the Universe? Do you think it

has wronged you? How happy can you be while you are holding a grudge against the Universe? This is the real issue. What you feel about the Universe shows you what you feel about yourself. Are you afraid of your anger? You will also be afraid of an angry Universe. The Universe isn't angry, but you will be afraid that it is.

Hating yourself and hating the Universe are the same thing. Loving yourself and loving the Universe are the same thing. Not forgiving the Universe is a heavy burden to carry. Why not lighten your load? In fact, why not get rid of it? If forgiving the Universe seems more than you can do, start by forgiving another person. Put down one suitcase at a time.

That is how you create harmony. It is also how you forgive.

Humbleness

She put the violin under her chin and, one by one, looked at the other musicians. Then, with a nod of her head that was almost invisible, the music began. Soft sounds from a guitar blended with the rich tones of a tenor sax. A drummer caressed cymbals with a steel brush. Through it all floated the thin, lilting melody of her violin. Together they moved through a realm so sweet, and sometimes so frantic, that it seemed to me they were all watching the same conductor.

If so, no one else saw him. The four musicians stood alone on the stage, each adding what only he or she could to a creation that could not have happened without all of them. A melody emerged, but no one person played it! They were each playing different melodies, but together they played a melody that was different still. The music became fuller and louder, richer and more complicated.

Then the guitar, the drums, and the saxophone began to play more softly. Moments later, an amazing sound came from my friend's violin. Soaring and dancing, tumbling and flowing, up and down and up again, it filled the room. Sweetly, then harshly, then softly again a new melody snaked itself away from the old, returned to it, and left it again. The guitar, saxophone, and drums played with it at every turn of its journey, sometimes supporting, sometimes challenging, and sometimes moving with it.

I had never heard jazz like this before. My friend finished her astounding performance with a flourish. I could not keep myself from clapping. Even before the applause faded, the guitarist began to rock gently on his stool, as if he were praying. Sweet notes slowly appeared as if from nowhere. The contrast of the guitar with the violin was gentle, yet stirring. In his own way, in his own time, he captivated us, excited us, delighted us, and soothed us. Beside his sounds, beneath his sounds, and through his sounds the sax, drums, and violin filled in all that was missing, and made space for all that he gave.

Again the room burst into applause. In turn, the saxophone player and the drummer stepped to the center of the musical circle. Each gave completely, led yet also joined, glowing in the musical light that the others shone on him or her. Applause exploded again and again as the music grew deeper and fuller. Then, slowly, they began to roll away the layers of complexity that each had contributed. Their sounds became softer, simpler and sweeter, until at last, in one lovely blending of notes and drumroll, they ended together.

The applause continued for a long time. The musicians nodded their acceptance to the audience and, I noticed, to one another. It seemed to me that they had completed a remarkable journey, and the shared experience of it had created a new and deeper bond between them, even though they played together often.

Could it be that each journey they took together—each concert—was different? Did each performance take them to unexplored depths, and bond them anew? I asked my friend, and she said, "Yes."

"Sometimes we experiment with themes that we have discovered, and sometimes we create something new. No concert is like another, and some of them are very different."

"How do you do that?" I asked.

She thought a moment, and then said, "I listen very hard so that what I play will be right. Not right in the sense of right or wrong, but right in the sense of what is needed. Together we find—or maybe we discover—or maybe we create—the groove. I can't tell you what that is, but I know when I am in it. We all do."

I listened quietly.

"Finding the groove requires two things from me," she added, as if thinking this through for the first time.

"What are they?" I asked.

"Complete self-responsibility, and complete surrender," she answered simply, nodding her head in approval of her clarity.

That is cooperation. It is also humbleness. Cooperation and humbleness always go together. Humbleness is seeing that everyone's path through the Earth school is as difficult as yours, and as important. It is not pretending that you are meek, or inferior. It is making the music together that cannot be made alone, and that cannot be made without the music that only you, alone, can make.

You can be humble only with friends. If you feel that you are less than another person, you will be intimidated, and frightened of making mistakes. If you feel that you are more important, you will not share everything that you can because you will not respect the person you are with. Can you give your best to someone you don't think can appreciate it? When you are friends, giving and receiving is the groove.

Everyone offers what he or she has. Everyone supports everyone else. Each steps to the microphone when it is his or her time, and each plays in the background when it is someone else's time. The music that you make together is special, and everyone knows it. You love to play it and to hear it.

Humble people feel that way all the time. They look at themselves as friends, and they look at others as friends. They cooperate naturally.

If you do not cooperate naturally, set the intention to cooperate. Then set it again and again.

Eventually, you will become humble without noticing it.

Clarity

I had never been to the summit in weather like this. The sky was flawless, the air was warm, and a soft breeze caressed us. Two miles below, cars crawled along a freeway like ants. A frozen lake in the crater of an adjoining mountain melted slowly into turquoise blue.

Everywhere I looked, unspoiled snow, glaciers, rocks warming in the sun, or blue to the horizon met my eyes. Talbot looked at me, and smiled. This was our third trip together. He had never seen conditions like these on the summit, either.

"It's good to be here with you," he said.

"It's good to be here, my friend," I replied with gratitude.

We had been climbing nine hours. There was no place left to climb. We had reached the top, where earth touches air for the last time. Not only were we on the summit, we were there with time to relax before starting down. I sat on the highest outcropping of this magnificent mountain. The sun warmed me, and my eyelids became heavy. I let them fall until I was in darkness.

The joy of being at the summit on this beautiful day washed over me. I gave thanks for my healthy body, and I thought of the many people who would never see this special place. I felt blessed. Slowly, my arms floated upward until they were above my head, fingers reaching toward the sky. It didn't take any effort to keep them there.

That's when it happened. I suddenly saw myself, the summit, and everything else differently. Before, I considered the summit to be a special place. It still was, but what I saw with my eyes closed was this: *Every place is the summit.* The grocery store is the summit. My home is the summit. School is the summit. There was no place that is not the summit.

This is clarity.

"Give me the best flower that you have," said a man to the florist.

"Every flower here is the best," replied the florist.

At these words, the man became enlightened.

This man had the same kind of experience that I had. It can happen to anyone. It can happen quickly, or slowly. It can happen when you are young, or when you are old. When you see, even for a moment, that what you thought was special is not more special than anything else, that is clarity. Clarity is seeing that every thing and every person is special, no matter what or who it is.

Clarity

A Navajo prayer says, "Beauty above me, Beauty below me, Beauty in front of me, Beauty behind me. All around me Beauty."

This is very different from the way that most people see. Most people think that some of their experiences are more beautiful than others, and that some people are more special than others.

Which way is real?

Imagine walking along a beach on a foggy day. You cannot see very far. You hear waves crashing on rocks, seagulls crying, and the wind blowing. Cold penetrates your clothes, and you shiver. Everywhere it is wet and gray. Sounds come from places you cannot see. You are frightened.

Now imagine that you are walking on the same beach, and the sun is shining. Sunlight sparkles on the water. Gulls fly through a cloudless sky. Cliffs with wildflowers tower above. Your feet sink into warm and welcome sand.

Which way of seeing is real? Clarity is seeing without the fog. It is getting your bearings in a well-lighted landscape. It is seeing without restrictions.

At one time or another, almost all of us have wakened in the night, frightened or crying. "Thank goodness!" we say when we realize where we are. Clarity is realizing where you are. It is exchanging a frightening experience of the dark for a wholesome experience of the light.

Clarity and sharing are twins. Where one goes, the other goes. When you share, you give something special to a special person. When you see clearly, everyone and everything is special. So each time you share, you learn to see clearly. The more you do it, the better at it you become.

When you take the time to be with someone, that is a

gift. When you share what you are feeling, even when you are afraid, that is a gift, too. Caring for someone is always a gift. It is the best gift that you can give. When you give gifts like these, you start to receive them. After a while, everything that you give and receive is a gift.

The trees and the mountains are also gifts. Who gave them? Who gave the animals, the birds, and your life? They are gifts from the Universe. Another gift that you get from the Universe is an experience that is perfect for you. This gift comes each moment from the time that you were born until you die.

You and the Universe create this gift together. You decide what it will be, and the Universe gives it to you. That is the Golden Rule—what you do to people, people do to you. It is also called karma. If you don't like what people do to you, you can change that by doing different things to them. That is how you and the Universe work together. Each moment you choose a new gift, and, when the time is right, the Universe gives it to you.

Each day brings gifts that you have ordered, and each day you place more orders. You do this by setting your intentions, and then acting on them. The Universe takes your orders, and delivers them. Everyone gets what she or he ordered. If you order fear, you get it. If you order love, you get it.

When you order, you share with the Universe. When your order is filled, the Universe shares with you. Complaining about your gifts is walking in the fog. Recognizing your gifts—and who ordered them—is walking in the sunshine.

Walking in the sunshine is clarity.

Love

The enormous redwood tree, ancient and failing, trembled. With a cracking, tearing sound, the unimaginable began to happen. Near the base, one side of the giant trunk began to crumple, like the first three floors of a collapsing building. On the opposite side, more than twenty feet away, a split suddenly appeared in the massive bark. The split grew vertically, slowly for a moment, then more rapidly as it widened.

Ever so slowly the mountain of wood, thousands of years old, began to move. In a canopy hundreds of feet above the forest floor, the top swayed in the wind, but this time, when it reached the end of its sway, it continued downward. The ripping, tearing sound grew until it was louder than the roar of a freight train. Tons of fiber, centuries in the making, started their last journey.

As the giant fell, it sheared huge branches, larger than oak trees, from neighboring redwoods. Down and down it fell with awesome force. Nothing could stop it now, and nothing did. It hit the forest floor, bounced once, and came to a final rest.

The thunder fell silent. In a few minutes, thousands of years of reaching toward the sun ended in one final embrace of the Earth. Slowly, the sounds of the forest returned. Insects buzzed, and leaves rustled in the breeze. Small animals reappeared cautiously, and larger animals began to move again.

This is part of a love story. The leaves, the trunk, the branches, and the roots were in love with each other.

Their love was continual. New leaves gently replaced those that turned brown. The redwood remained green for centuries, but none of the leaves on it were centuries old. The bark loved the roots, and the roots loved the branches. The trunk held them together, and the leaves nourished them all.

The love story of the redwood tree had other characters in it, too. It loved the Earth and the sky. It reached for both from the moment it sprouted to the moment of its dramatic fall. It loved the birds that nested in its branches, the animals that sheltered beneath it, and the insects that fed from its bark. They were one family, full and complete.

Does this story sound familiar? It should. You see it everywhere you look, inside and out.

The cells in your body love each other. Your blood loves your heart and your lungs. Your spine loves your brain. Your body is a love story that continues day after day. Every part of your body gives what other parts need, and receives from them what it needs. You are a walking, talking story of love.

Every love story is part of a larger love story, and every love story, no matter how large or small, has endless stories of love within it. The Universe has countless galaxies. Each galaxy has countless stars. Each star has countless molecules, atoms, and subatomic particles dancing within it, becoming one another, splitting apart in different ways, and coming together again.

The biggest love story has no beginning, like we do, and like redwood trees do. It doesn't have an end, either. We are parts of that story. Sometimes when we glimpse it, we are awed and delighted. Scientists call this big love story "interconnectivity." Nothing exists without everything else. When we think that anything can exist without us, it is because we are only seeing a small part of a few love stories. Sometimes, we don't even see our own.

The love stories happen whether we see them or not. The love story of the tree does not end when the tree falls. A new chapter begins. The tree decays and gives all of itself back to the Earth. Insects devour it, and birds eat the insects. Bees make hives in it, and bears eat honey from the hives. Even when the tree disappears, the story is not over. More trees appear, and more insects, birds, and animals, too. When the forest disappears, the story does not end. Even when the Earth ends, which it will do some day, the story does not end. It has no ending.

Love and reverence go together. When you see the big love story, you realize that you are in everyone's story, and everyone and everything is in yours. Even people you haven't met yet are part of your story, and you are part of theirs. Their suffering is part of your story, and their happiness, too. Your suffering and happiness are part of theirs. The big love story includes everything.

When your story becomes everyone's story, and everyone's story becomes yours, that is love.

Trust

"Ask the Creator for what you want," they told her, "and the Creator will always answer you."

They had told her that since she was a baby. Now she was almost seven.

"I asked the Creator for something," she said one morning.

"What did you ask for, darling?" they asked.

"For snow on my birthday!" she said, giggling.

Her parents looked at each other in alarm. The little girl's birthday was in July, and they lived in the desert. It is very hot in July in the desert.

Two weeks later the little girl spoke about her birthday again.

"I want a party with all of my friends," she announced.

Now they were very alarmed, but they arranged the party. Everyone came, had a wonderful time, and left. There was no snow, but the little girl didn't appear to be sad.

"Are you disappointed that the Creator didn't answer you?" they asked her gently.

"He did answer me," she replied. "He said, 'No!'"

Some people call the Creator the Universe. They think they know how the Universe works, like the parents of the little girl. They are always disappointed, and trying to understand why things happen. They are happy with some answers the Universe gives them, and unhappy with others.

"Why would the Universe do this to me?" they ask.

"This isn't fair!" they say.

The difference between these people and the little girl is trust. She is happy with any answer the Universe gives. They aren't. They think they know how the Universe should be. When it isn't that way, they get upset.

Have you ever been so worried about something—like an exam—that you can't think about anything else? If your car won't start on exam day, you get frightened. If you leave your notes at home, you get angry. You want to pass your exam, but the Universe wants you to do other things.

Your exam is important, but learning about fear and anger is important, too. That is more important to the Universe than your exam. You can do it all at the same time. When your car won't start, you learn about fear. When you leave your notes at home, you learn about anger. When you take your exam, you see how much you learned in class.

In the Hindu tradition, Indra is a god who runs the

Heavens. One day he decided to visit the Earth. He didn't come back. After a while, the other gods got worried. They sent messengers to look for him.

At last one of the messengers found him. Indra had become a pig.

"Indra!" cried the messenger. "You must come back. The Heavens are coming apart!"

"Come back?" said Indra, amazed. "I can't come back! I have a she-pig and five piglets."

Indra forgot who he was. The messenger wanted him to remember.

When you think of the Universe as a partner that always helps you remember the most important things, that is trust.

A coach knows more than her players. Think of the Universe as your coach. To play your best, you need to listen. If you don't trust her, you won't take her advice. Sooner or later—after a lot of bad plays—you will start listening. Why not save yourself the time?

Trusting the Universe does that.

The Universe always brings your attention to what is most important. It wants you to pay attention to what is happening in your life. When you do that, you are listening to your coach. You don't stop doing your part. You don't stop training, or playing your best. You start listening, and your game gets better.

The game is your life. The Universe wants you to learn from the happy things that happen to you. It wants you to learn from the painful things, too. Your part is to be aware, use your intuition, and set your intentions. Then be like the little girl who lived in the desert, and see what happens next. You may think you know what is best for you, but the Universe knows what you don't. Indra insisted on being a pig. What are you insisting on?

The Universe is not coaching you to be frightened, angry or sad. It is coaching you to become all that you are, like the messenger from Indra's home, Heaven.

Knowing that is trust.

PART III

What It Looks Like

The Old Male

"They're coming! They're coming!" shouted little Harry Song Hawk.

In the distance horses appeared against the pale evening sky. From every tepee women and children emerged into the sharp, cold air, their faces drawn and tight.

"Can you see?" asked Kate Bloody Knife to her daughter.

"They are all there," said the younger woman, squinting her eyes, and counting quickly. "Thirty-four men."

"Thank you, Great Spirit," the old woman whispered, relief flowing through her frail body for the first time in ten nights.

The horses drew closer, slowly approaching the children and women waiting patiently.

Suddenly George Walking Shield's fist, holding his spear and eagle feather, shot high into the air. His victory cry thundered across the empty snow, filling the village with his joyous voice. The women wept with joy, and the children leaped with excitement.

Beside Walking Shield, thirty-three men, young and old, smiled with pride. They, too, thanked the Great Spirit with every strike of horses' hooves on the frozen ground.

"Bring wood for the fire," said Ruth Bloody Knife to her son. The boy bounded toward the trees behind them, jumping with delight. Then, handing her daughter a small gourd, Ruth said with a smile, "Fill this with water." As the girl danced toward the stream, Ruth, like her mother, relaxed for the first time since her husband had mounted his horse and, with his uncles and brothers, ridden into the frozen morning almost half a moon ago.

"Tonight we eat! At last," she sighed to herself. "Tonight we eat."

Would you like to be like George Walking Shield and his brothers and uncles? Until recently, almost every man and every boy would say yes. That is because Walking Shield and those who rode beside him magnificently filled the role that every man was born to fill—until recently. That is to provide for those he loves, and to protect them, with his life, if necessary. It is to keep his family safe, and give his children all that they need to grow strong and healthy.

Billions of men have filled this role. Billions more have tried, some with more success than others. It has been the goal of every son and the completion of every father. Here is a modern version of the same story.

"When will Father come?" asked Marie, putting her doll into its bed for the fifth time. "I miss him."

"I miss him, too, darling," said Nancy, gently stroking her daughter's silky brown hair.

Upstairs the voices of cartoon characters drifted from the television through the hall. Now and then Tommy cried with excitement. In the kitchen soup simmered, filling the house with a delicious fragrance.

Suddenly the front door flew open, and there was Father, a newspaper tucked under his left elbow, holding a sack of groceries in each arm. The cold swirled in beside him.

"Daddy, Daddy!" shouted Tommy, running down the stairs. Marie was already clinging to his right leg. The sack on the left began to tear.

"Hi, pumpkin," he smiled, trying to keep the groceries upright.

Nancy came to the rescue. "Welcome, darling," she said, her eyes twinkling, giving him a kiss on the cheek. He beamed.

"It's good to be home," he smiled, giving her the tearing sack. "It's good to be home."

Can you see that the two stories are the same? Both are noble. The protector has returned. The provider has come. All is well. All is safe. He is here. He is here.

This role is ancient. It is as old as humankind. It is the heart of what it has meant to be male. Without the provider and the protector, humanity would not exist. The protector has kept it safe. The provider has kept it warm and fed. He is the father, the uncle, and the grandfather. Whatever his mate and his children, his nieces and nephews, and his grandchildren need, he provides. When danger is near, so is he, always between it and them. Nothing is more important to him. They are the reason he was born, and the reason he lives. They can depend on him. As long as he has breath in his body, they can depend on him. He is there for them.

This is an especially beautiful role because it does not exist by itself. It is half of a larger picture.

The other half is magnificent, too.

The Old Female

Shiszuko looked into Miyako's beautiful almond-shaped eyes, and caressed her coal black hair. The tiny, soft body in her arms twisted as its little arms extended outward and its delicate yet strong feet kicked in short, jerky movements. Miyako closed her eyes tightly, and then opened them again even more widely, exploring the new world that had become her own. They turned toward Shiszuko, and fixed themselves on her.

Shiszuko was stunned. The penetrating gaze of her newest-born seemed to go through her. She wished she could see what it saw. A new life had been born, as different from her other children as she was from her sisters, from her brothers, from her husband, from everyone. How could a child, so tender, so defenseless, only hours old, be so present and unique? She saw in the dark eyes still fixed on her own the power of a life already unfolding, like a seed growing toward the great tree that it will become.

Miyako's expression changed. Shiszuko felt it the moment she saw it. Gently she brought the tiny body upward. Its mouth touched her left breast, and Miyako began to suck. Her needs expressed and fulfilled, the tiny infant became content, gently, rhythmically drinking her mother's milk. Not only Miyako was nourished. The deep satisfaction that Shiszuko felt every time she nursed her children rose in her again. She looked lovingly at the nursing child and felt the familiar love engulf her. Another tiny body, another precious soul, another deep friend that she would love throughout her life had arrived.

Her journey had begun anew, again. She would always know Miyako's needs. She would always feel her pain, and thrill at her joy. She would explore the world with her, and marvel at their differences, as she did with her two sons. Now their family was five—she and her husband, Miyako, and Miyako's brothers.

More would come. She felt that in her heart. Patience grew in her as her family grew. All was unfolding as it should, as it needed to. The wonder of her children and her life flowed over her. She closed her eyes, like a lioness in the warmth of the sun, and began to drift. Her body relaxed for the first time since the birth. She was thinking of her new daughter, her sons, and their father when sleep came at last. Her body knew enough to rest while it could. There was much more to do.

Much more.

The Old Female

Shiszuko will continue to nurse Miyako throughout her life, providing her with what she needs as a girl, as she grows into womanhood, as an adult, and as a mother herself. Shiszuko's life will grow richer and deeper, stronger and more clear, as she moves through her time on the Earth, supporting her children, watching them grow, loving them ever more deeply. She will become a well of strength to them, a fountain that never dries, a star that always shines. This is her goal and her fulfillment. She was born to do these things, and she will. Nothing can stop her.

This role is ancient, too. Billions of women have lived it, and billions more will. They are the mothers, the aunts, and the grandmothers of the human family. They are there for us. As long as there is breath in their bodies, they are there for us. They complete the picture. The old male completes the picture, too. Together, they are the wellspring of human life.

The old male and the old female are to each other what the moon is to the sun, the sand is to the sea, and the mountains are to the sky. They go together. Together they reveal a design that is larger than both of them. Together they accomplish a goal that they cannot reach alone. Everything they do serves this goal. It is to keep alive the human species. They need each other, and human life needs them.

The old male and the old female were born to serve this goal, their lives serve this goal, and so does their special form of union.

Marriage

Barbara approached Nathan as though she were floating. The look of awe on his face told her that she must be in a special state. She felt that way. All she could see were the people in front of her. Her beloved Nathan, his friend, her friends, and the priest. She took her place before them. It seemed to her that she had always known that she would stand here, with these people, doing what she was doing now.

The priest spoke, but she didn't hear him until he turned toward her.

"Barbara"—she held her gaze on Nathan as he spoke— "will you have Nathan as your husband, to love him, comfort him, honor him, and keep him in sickness and in health, forsaking all others to be faithful to him as long as you live?"

She must have spoken well, because the priest turned toward Nathan and asked him the same questions. Her heart was doing the speaking for her. It filled her, spilled over into the large room, and made it radiant.

"The marriage of Nathan and Barbara unites a family and creates a new one," said the priest, now speaking to the people in front of them. "Will you do everything in your power to uphold and care for these two people in their marriage?"

"Yes," the room itself seemed to answer.

Barbara saw the mouth of the priest moving, but she was still not listening to him. She was listening to her heart. From deep inside her came words, and she spoke them. "I, Barbara, take you, Nathan, to be my husband, to have and to hold, for better or worse, richer or poorer, in sickness and in health, to love and obey until death do us part. This is my solemn vow." Her voice carried to the farthest corner, filling every space, declaring her commitment from this moment until the moment of her death.

Nathan's face was somber. He spoke the same words, each coming into the holy space like cut crystal, sharp and clear. She had never seen him so present, so big, so unshakable. She knew that he spoke the truth. So did everyone else.

Nathan slipped his ring onto her finger. She carefully, deliberately, placed the ring that she brought to this special place, at this special time, to this special man, on his finger.

"Those whom God has joined together let no one put asunder," spoke the priest. "I now pronounce you man and wife."

The room burst into celebration.

A contract as old as humankind had been signed with the heart. A new family was created, mirroring the countless families that had come before them. A husband and wife had joined in order to do what husbands and wives have always done—help each other to survive and have children. Barbara loves Nathan, and Nathan loves Barbara. They long to share a home and make it their nest. Like birds, they will hatch offspring, in their own way, and like birds, their young will leave the nest to fly on their own. This is not an easy job.

Both will work very hard. Nathan will earn the money to buy food, clothes, show their children as much of the world as he can, and educate them. Barbara will nurture them continually. She will clean the nest and prepare the food. She will meet with teachers and tend the hurts. Both of them will model the roles that their children will play someday. These are the roles of the old male and the old female.

The old male, the old female, and marriage go together. The old male and the old female need each other to do what they were born to do. The old male needs to provide and protect. The old female needs to bear children and raise them. Marriage is the way they do these things.

The old male and the old female must marry and have children the same way that birds must fly toward warm weather for the winter and bison must drift toward green prairies. It is a part of who they are. It is at the core of their being. It ensures the survival of humankind.

Every marriage, in every culture, bonds an old male and

an old female. It is designed for them, performed by them, and launches them into action. It declares a new family, forbids anyone to disrupt it, and enrolls the support of all.

When they marry, Barbara and Nathan commit to support each other when they are sick and when they are healthy, when they have money and when they don't. They commit to stay together during hard times. For them only one thing can change that—one or both of them must die.

This is the most powerful commitment that an old male and an old female can make. They are five-sensory. They cannot see beyond their deaths. The world they live in is limited to what they can taste, touch, hear, smell and see. When they die, they can't do these things. That is why a commitment until death is the most meaningful one they can make.

This arrangement has kept us evolving for tens of thousands of years. The old female bears and raises children. The old male protects them and provides for them. Marriage brings them together to do these things.

What happens when multisensory perception enters the picture?

The New Female

"Ladies and Gentlemen, the next President of the United States!"

It was not an exaggeration. Both parties had come to an unprecedented support of the same candidate. Pessimists had feared the collapse of the two-party system. Optimists had painted pictures of a new era in American politics. Now everyone was watching in fascination.

The great hall exploded into a frenzy of banners, music, cheers, and exhilaration. She walked into the spotlights and took her position behind the podium, smiling her radiant smile, and waving with her right hand held high. The thunderous exuberance went on and on. Her grace and strength combined into a beautiful picture of poise and balance. She nodded her acceptance and her appreciation to the beloved audience before her, and the millions of people watching her on television across the nation and around the world.

No one in the history of democracy had referred to an electorate as beloveds. Diana did it naturally, and no one seemed to mind, strange as it first sounded. She had done it as a mayor, as a senator, and as a candidate for the presidency. It was clear from her radiant smile that she continued to see the electorate as her beloveds now that she was, in effect, the president-elect of the United States of America.

At last the applause began to subside. As if everyone were following the same signal, the delegates began to focus their attention on the solitary figure on the stage before them. Around the country and around the world, millions of people did the same thing.

Diana waited patiently, listening to her inner sense of timing. Her black dress accentuated her black skin. Her ebony hair, styled differently yet again, shone in the brilliant light. At last Diana—the same Diana who brought peace to the streets of her once violent city, who had united congressmen and congresswomen in ways that none had dreamed possible—began to speak.

"My dear brothers and sisters," she began, "we stand at a crossroads, again." It was the beginning of a speech that historians would unanimously praise, and students of politics would read again and again through the years. Amazingly, she spoke without notes.

"Within us new life is emerging. A new springtime has arrived. We are a part of it, but no longer a part that stands alone. A new era in American history has arrived. We are a petal on the blossom of a great flower. Our struggles are now blending with the struggles of others, and our fulfillment is now flowing into the fulfillment of others.

"We Americans are pioneers. Our ancestors come from every culture. In our blood flows the blood of every brother and every sister. In us grow the roots of appreciation for all, because we come from all. The history of our country is brief. The history of our origins is timeless, and contains the histories of all cultures.

"Now we face a new frontier—the frontier of interdependence. We are excellent at exploring new frontiers. It is our destiny to explore this one. America is uniquely prepared for this challenge. We have skills to offer, and experiences to share. Yet the frontier of interdependence cannot be explored alone. It is not a frontier of mountains and prairies. It is a frontier of compassion and cocreativity. It is a frontier that now stands before every woman and every man, in every culture, at every moment."

Diana continued for another twenty minutes. "It is the role of the American people," she said, "to model interdependence, and to live it in every way." At another time she said, "History and our hearts have now joined cause—and that cause is Life."

When she finished, there was a long silence. Then the applause began. It grew steadily as Diana's words sank home. Suddenly it became thunderous again. In the months and years to come, Diana's words would sink even deeper.

Does this picture seem unreal to you? Can a woman excel in a domain that has been dominated by men, such as politics, and bring to it all of her compassion and perceptions as a female? If you look around, you will see that this is happening all the time. The captain of your airplane, the chief executive officer of your company, and, for some, the president of your country, is a woman. The carpenter who builds your house, the truck driver who brings food to your grocery store, and the mail carrier on your street are women.

These women are not like women of the past. They do not consider themselves limited in any way, and they are not.

They follow their hearts. If they choose to become construction workers, they do. When they are drawn to the business world, they enter it. If they want to become a professional, they go to school. If they want to have children, they have children.

This is very different from the old female. The role of the old female is to have children and raise them. She does not have another role, and she is not drawn to one. Only having children and raising her family satisfies her. She does this very well. She can't do anything else, and she doesn't want to do anything else.

The new female can do what the old female does—bear children and raise them—if she chooses. She can also do anything else. That is the difference between the old female and the new female. The new female can do anything. The old female can't. The old female only wants to have children and raise them. That is the life that she is drawn to, and it fulfills her. Nothing else calls her as strongly. She doesn't think about creating a business, or becoming a professional, or driving a truck. That is for her husband.

The new female is not limited in any way. She is as competent as Diana, the president-elect, and as compassionate. She yearns to give the gifts that she was born to give, and she does what is necessary to give them. Where her heart leads, she goes. No one defines her role for her. She is on a spiritual journey. Authentic power is her destination.

This is new to the human experience. Every culture has stories about women such as these, but never before have such women appeared in all places, in all cultures, at the same time. That is happening now. Females who do not see themselves as limited in any way—and are not limited in any way—are showing up everywhere.

When they do, big changes happen.

Old Male Meets New Female— Version I

"I don't want to live like this anymore!" Her eyes were red from crying. She desperately tried now to say what needed to be said, what came from the heart she had so long buried. She looked at him directly.

"You don't know how you speak to me. You don't have any idea. You are not being respectful, and I don't want that anymore."

John stared at her. His heart felt as cold as ice to him. His jaw tightened and his eyes narrowed.

"Don't look at me like that!" she half pleaded, half warned. "I love you, but I am not going to take that from you or anyone again."

"What did I say?" he shot back. "That we can't go to the movies? Is that worth this argument?"

"It's the way you said it," she tried to explain. "It's not what you said."

John's exasperation reached the boiling point.

"Nothing I say meets your approval anymore! You don't like the way I speak to you. You don't like the way I look at you."

"I don't like it when you don't respect me."

Her eyes were becoming as icy as his. Then they flared with anger.

John almost stepped backward. Her rage surprised him, as it had last week and again yesterday. He was not used to seeing her furious. He never knew that she could be. He felt humiliation flow through him. If she spoke to him this way now, she would speak to him like this in front of others. His shame at the thought turned his face red.

"I pay for this house," he reminded her, his voice rising. "I pay for our food. I pay for our clothes. I pay for everything, and I work hard to do it. Don't you think that's worth a little thanks?"

Carol backed away, not out of fear, but out of hopelessness. Her love and her anger were more than she could hold at the same time. To her surprise, her anger refused to give way, and it refused to go underground.

"I start school next week," she said, abruptly changing the subject.

"You do not," replied John. "Who will watch the children? Who will keep this house clean? Who will cook?"

"We'll do it together," she tried again, "or we'll find someone to help us."

"And who will pay?" he cried. "Do you think school is

free? Do you really believe the world needs another archi-
tect? Your children need you. I need you. What is going on
with you?"

John cannot understand the changes in Carol. She is a
puzzle to him, and a very unpleasant one. His world is coming apart. Everything he planned and worked for is slipping
away. She is not keeping her part of the bargain. She is not
holding up her side. He is hurt and angry. Carol is no
longer the woman he married. She promised to love,
honor, and obey—obey him. They are a team, but she cannot see that, and so the team is dissolving.

His anguish and his anger blend into a single, painful experience. He can no longer distinguish between them.
Where there is one, there is the other. What will become of
their children? His heart breaks at the thought. Like water
flowing through his fingers, the life that he longs for is dis-
appearing. All of his plans. All of his hopes. All of his dreams.
He can do nothing to stop it. Where is the Carol that he
married, his wife, his companion, his playmate, the mother
of his children?

The point of no return has come for Carol. She does not
want to face it, but she knows it in her heart. Life with
John has become a tomb. Daily she goes through the mo-
tions of belonging in it, but she no longer does. She will
find a way to care for their children. She will always do
that, somehow, some way. Inside her a huge shift is occur-
ring, like two tectonic plates rearranging themselves. An
earthquake is shaking her life, and it has just begun. It will
not stop until the shift is complete, and the tension is gone.
Her marriage is the fault line.

When she thinks of school, her heart sings. She is challenged by the thought and attracted by the idea. Her first trip to the campus is terrifying. No faces are familiar. She is older than most of the students. Yet she belongs there, and she is grateful. Her new life calls to her, and she answers with a YES she has never felt before. Her therapy with John is now to ease the pain of their separation. She has no thought of returning. Her vision has gone elsewhere. She is on a new path, although she can see only one step of it at a time.

Deep inside, she knows that something special is happening. She thinks that her wings are unfolding, but she cannot yet see that she is flying.

Old Male Meets New Female—
Version II

"I don't want to live like this anymore!" Her eyes were red from crying. She desperately tried now to say what needed to be said, what came from the heart she had so long buried. She looked at him directly.

"You don't know how you speak to me. You don't have any idea. You are not being respectful, and I don't want that anymore."

John stared at her. His jaw was set. His eyes narrowed.

"Don't look at me like that!" she half pleaded, half warned. "I love you, but I am not going to take that from you or anyone again."

There was an awkward silence. John struggled hard to listen. His anger battled with his confusion. Why this outbreak, again? What was he doing that was so horrible?

"What did I say?" he asked, on the defensive. "That we can't go to the movies? Is that worth this argument?"

"It's the way you said it," she tried to explain. "It's not what you said."

His struggle intensified. How had he spoken? How could that be a problem? He felt wronged, but he also felt vulnerable.

"Nothing I say meets your approval anymore!" he said lamely. His words sounded empty to him, but he continued anyway. "You don't like the way I speak to you. You don't like the way I look at you."

"I don't like it when you don't respect me."

The silence returned. He looked away. There was something in her eyes that burned through him. They had never been angry with each other like this. Now they argued week after week. She was at the end of her patience, and John knew it.

Suddenly Carol's eyes flared with anger.

"You are not respecting me!" she screamed.

John almost stepped backward. He felt humiliation rush through him. If she spoke to him like this when they were alone, she would speak to him like this in front of others. His shame at the thought turned his face red. He felt himself stiffen. He prepared to shout louder, to overpower her anger with his own, when something unexpected happened. As he looked at her, trembling with rage in front of him, his heart softened. She had become fearless. He admired that. He liked the feeling of admiring his partner.

Suddenly his heart opened like a flower. He was flooded with a new understanding. He had not seen Carol this angry before because no one had. Her rage flowed underground, deep beneath her fear and shame. Now it had exploded through the surface of her life and into his own. In that moment, John knew that he was a very special person to Carol, and he knew why. He was the first person she trusted enough to show her rage. He felt like cheering.

He forgot to be humiliated. He listened with a new interest. What else would surface? It seemed to him they had entered a special place together, where everything is very real. A moment ago he was hurt and angry at Carol. Now he supported her with all his heart.

A part of John wanted to say, "I pay for this house. I pay for our food. I pay for everything, and I work hard to do it. Don't you think that's worth a little thanks?"

He didn't. He didn't say anything. He *wanted* to receive her rage, and to let her feel his love. This was a new experience for John. He didn't realize it at the time, but his life was changing. For the first time, he forgot about himself and listened to an angry person, really listened.

This is how it works. When the new female emerges in a relationship, the old male either leaves or begins to change, too. His partner helps him, if he allows her. Then their relationship becomes very different.

The moment seemed to last forever. Carol stood with her fists clenched, glaring wildly at him. John stood across the small room, motionless and silent.

"I start school next week," she said, defiantly.

John nodded his wordless agreement. Of course she would, he realized. Nothing could stop her. Her heart had found a path, and she was following it. He felt curiously excited. He had never had a partner like this before. The rules were changing, and so was he. He knew that he was in unexplored territory.

"We will work out something," he heard himself say. Then his fear returned. How could they? He needed to work, and someone had to watch the children. More than that, he feared losing Carol and losing his family. What would she do next? Would she want to be with someone like him, now that she had a calling in her life? Would anyone?

"Of course we will," he heard Carol say. The softness in her voice surprised him. Her face had changed, too. She was looking at him with a mixture of curiosity and love.

He didn't know what they would do next, but he knew that they would do it together.

So did she.

The New Male

The terminal was busier than usual. People were everywhere, rushing or waiting on their way to somewhere else. The lines were long. The seats were few. In one crowded area, a young man gently rocked a soft bundle in his arms. I could see him whispering to it. He must have felt me, because he looked in my direction with an easy, flowing movement of his head.

We smiled the way people do when they share something special. His love for the infant he was carrying washed over me. I became a part of it. Suddenly the busy airport changed into a warm and friendly place. The young man's love for the baby in his arms transformed me from a weary traveler into a fellow soul on a journey into intimacy. He was not worried about time. Nothing distracted him. His baby was enough. He delighted in it, watching its every movement.

He appeared to be someone who wakes up early, changes diapers often, and makes the meals. I felt safe with him. A woman joined him. She held tickets in one hand and a purse in the other. She smiled at him and then at their child.

Have you seen men like this? Men who are tender yet competent, loving yet perceptive. Men who are nurturing yet courageous. Men who do not try to please others, yet are generous. Men who know what they feel. Men who are not confined by the role of the old male. Men who follow their hearts.

If not, you soon will. They are appearing in every age group, culture, race, and economic category. They are the new males. They are not new versions of the old male. They are a new creation in the human experience. They are redefining masculinity.

The old male provides and protects. That is all that he can do. That is all that he was designed to do. Providing and protecting are his reasons for being and his fulfillment. The new male can do anything. He can provide and protect, and he can be provided for and protected. He can be a corporate executive or cook for his children. He is not confined to the roles that his culture has created for him. He can be a warrior, executive, plumber, secretary, nurse, or anything else. He is free to explore any path he chooses.

The new male loves Life. He loves the old and the young. He loves animals and plants, people and the Earth. He cares for the sick, nurtures the young, and visits the lonely. He cries when he is sad and laughs when he is happy. His emotions flow through him like a river. Neither career nor profession can confine him. No rule can keep him from his heart. He is emotionally whole.

There have always been men like this who have brought love into action, cared deeply, and lived their lives that way—but never before have such men appeared in all cultures, in all places, at the same time. That is what is happening now. New males are emerging everywhere—in the young and in the old, in the rich and in the poor.

They are changing everything as they do.

Old Female Meets New Male—
Version I

He had finally done it.

Marjorie's face contorted. "Only twelve more years!" she cried. "You would have retired in twelve years!"

Fred knew that.

"You had everything, and you threw it away! You could have dug in every garden in this city for the rest of your life and never had to worry about a thing. Now what are you going to do?"

"Start advertising," he said. "I'm ready."

"You're ready!" she mocked him. "What about the rest of the world? How many people do you think are going to hire a middle-aged ex-professor to plant bushes in their yards?"

"Design their landscape," Fred corrected.

"Can't you understand?" she pleaded, as she had before. Tears came to her eyes.

"Marjorie," he said, coming toward her tenderly. "Biology is boring. It's talk about. I want to do. This world is alive, and the part of it I love best is growing in the ground. Now I can do what I have been teaching all my life. I can become a part of that world, work with it, learn from it, and give people beautiful homes at the same time."

"This is embarrassing," she said. "My husband, the professor, digging in people's yards, like a gardener."

"I am more than a gardener," said Fred. "And don't forget, I'll be writing my books."

"Books about what?" she exploded. "How to grow potatoes in a city? How to sit in the dirt all day?"

"Marjorie," Fred tried again. He reached toward her, but she folded her arms across her stomach and turned away.

"You are a fool!" she hissed. "You are a fool, and you don't even know it."

Marjorie is paralyzed with fear. She is partway through a journey that requires two, and her partner has left her. Everything she lives for is in jeopardy. He pays the bills—or did. He buys the food—or did. Now what will happen? He is not young. He has students and responsibilities. He has tenure. He *had* tenure.

She thought of the faculty club she would no longer see, the graduations she would no longer attend, and the students who adored her husband. Despair gripped her. Her entire life was coming apart.

Fred didn't see things that way. He felt like a young man. His step was lighter and his smile was contagious. Only Marjorie marred his happiness. He wanted her company. He longed for it, but his longing was already beginning to fade. They had shared so much together. He wanted to share more, but he could not. She was the enemy of all that now called him. To have Marjorie and his new world was his dream. That dream already was adapting itself to Marjorie's decision.

Long before she filed for divorce, Fred's new life was taking form. New friends were flowing into it, and new challenges were drawing him. New satisfactions appeared, like flowers in the spring. Fred had moved into new territory, and nothing—including his love for Marjorie—could draw him back into the old.

A new world was being born, and it was being born inside Fred.

Old Female Meets New Male— Version II

"I sold the business." Michael smiled. "I'm a free man."

Ruth was not smiling.

"Charles organized it," he said. "An employee buyout. They're in, and I'm out."

For twelve years she had supported Michael—while he studied to become an insurance broker, while he struggled to establish his business, and while he hired one, then another, and then another agent. Now he had the largest insurance agency in the state—or he had until now. No other agency sold more. No other was as well known, or as admired. All of it had been Michael's. Now all of it was his employees'.

"They will double the business in five years," he continued, still smiling. "Then I'll take my equity."

What about *now?* thought Ruth angrily.

Anyone with a nose for profit—and Michael had one when she met him—could have come out of this set for life.

Her words exploded out at last. "What about our plans? How are we going to live?"

"We'll get an apartment," said Michael, "and I'll start writing."

She glared at him.

"It's happening, darling," Michael said joyfully, as though she were smiling back. "It's happening at last!"

Michael was moving into his dream. Ruth was moving into her nightmare. She had promised to love and obey him, but he was not the man she had married. She felt he had gone insane. For years he had threatened to sell his business. Now he had sold it. Her worst fear had happened.

"Why?" she snapped, looking at him fiercely. "Why?"

"So we can live the lives we were born to live," he answered, trying to explain yet again how he felt. "So we can follow our passion. There is more waiting for us than a retirement banquet. Let's find what it is. Let's explore this life together."

Ruth continued to fume, but a new feeling began to mingle with her anger. She tried hard to ignore it, but Michael's words were exciting her in some way.

What was exciting about leaving their house? What was exciting about an apartment, about not knowing what Michael would do each day? What was exciting about not knowing what *she* would do each day? This was not what she had expected from her marriage. Yet she had the funny feeling that she was becoming a young girl again.

Slowly, like a view of an ocean emerging through a thinning fog, she realized something. For the first time, she had asked Michael, "Why?" and listened to him. His answer surprised her.

This is how it happens. When a new male emerges into a relationship, the relationship breaks up, or the old female changes. She leaves, or she begins to see new possibilities.

Michael and Ruth spoke long into the night, as they used to do, listening to each other as they had not done in years. Michael spoke of his love for writing, and of his love for her. Ruth spoke of her aspirations, some of them old, and some of them surprising and new. They both spoke of their fears.

Slowly, their old life together began to seem small. Even their house began to feel smaller. As Ruth looked at Michael, radiant in the early morning, she saw him in a way that she had never seen him. It seemed to her that he was a pioneer, a friend, and a collaborator of the heart.

She wondered where a collaboration with him might lead.

A New Way of
Relating

"Did you call her to see if there was a chance of getting back together?"

Linda sat by me at the dinner table, waiting for my answer. I didn't know what to say. That is exactly why I had made the call. The one person I didn't want to know this was Linda.

I was torn. A part of me wanted to reconstruct my broken engagement. For five years I had thought about my ex-fiancée. I had moved forward through the pain. I had learned about myself, but my heart still reached for the dreams that we had shared. I needed to know if they were still possible, so I called her.

My ex-fiancée's anger greeted me when she answered, and it was the last thing I heard when we hung up. There was no room for my question in our conversation. Mostly I listened, and she expressed her anger. The dreams we once shared were not a possibility, but I still longed for them. Now Linda was asking me about that question.

The candle lit her face softly. She waited patiently for my answer, looking at me. I wanted to tell her the truth, to explain everything—the five years of pain and growth, the longing for my former fiancée, and the embarrassment of admitting that now. I also didn't want to upset my relationship with Linda. I didn't know exactly what that relationship was, but I knew it was important to me. We had become friends, and then companions, over the last half year. Slowly, I had begun to suspect that we were more than friends and companions.

I looked forward to her company. We talked about things that were important to me—about inner and outer struggles. We helped each other to understand our challenges, she hers, and I mine. Now, six months after we met, it occurred to me that I might be in a "relationship," but one unlike any I had experienced. There was no romance. There was no sexual intimacy. Sometimes I annoyed her, and at other times, she annoyed me. Sometimes I felt uncomfortable during our conversations, and I wondered why. Other times, her company was a delight for me.

This was the "relationship" that had formed, and I enjoyed exploring it with Linda. Linda knew about my ex-fiancée, and my high regard for her, but she didn't know much more. I knew that my longing for her was bringing me to a crossroads. I wanted to explore my new "relationship" with Linda, but I didn't want to close the door on the possibility of a life with my former fiancée, if one existed. That is why I had to call.

I had mentioned the call to Linda, but not what it was about. Linda knew immediately, and gently asked me her question. Now I sat in the silence with her, extremely uncomfortable and frightened. If I didn't tell Linda the truth, it would be the first time. The thought of lying to her made me feel sick. Yet how could I possibly say, "I miss my ex-fiancée. I called to ask if there is any possibility of a reconciliation. I needed to know that before opening my heart to you."

The stakes were so high. If I lied to Linda, I would destroy the very thing I loved most about our relationship. If I didn't, I might lose her as a friend and a companion, not to mention losing what I felt might be ahead for us.

I decided to tell her what was in my heart. I told her how much I loved my former fiancée, and how much I had missed her. I told her all that I had learned from our experiences together, and from my experiences afterward. I told her of my embarrassment.

I had never felt so vulnerable. I didn't realize until that moment how important Linda was to me. I prepared for her to get up, put down her napkin, and leave. I braced myself for a life without the conversations that I enjoyed so much, and for the hole in my life that Linda's absence would leave. I held my breath, waiting for the worst.

Linda continued looking at me, thoughtfully. At last she said, "I am glad you told me these things. Now I can love her, too."

I never felt relief like the relief I felt when I heard Linda's words. I was not only relieved that she was still in my life. I was relieved that I could say what was most important to me without causing a catastrophe. I had said the unspeakable, and we were still sitting at the table, and still growing together. I had probed my heart and tested my courage, and all with Linda. What an amazing thing this "relationship" was. I had entered new territory. The idea that we could continually explore this territory together was exciting to me. In my heart, I knew that we would.

Linda and I had discovered a thrilling way to grow together—to say what is most frightening. My appreciation of her deepened. I felt safe with her. I thought that she would recoil from my thoughts. Instead, she understood my fears. Before I shared them, I felt ashamed. Afterward, I felt healed. It was not shameful to feel lonely, or to long for the past! My longing for my former fiancée did not subside for several years, but it stopped being frightening to me. I no longer had to hide an important part of myself from Linda, or anyone else.

My sharing, and Linda's listening, created more intimacy between us. I trusted her, and she trusted me. Now this kind of sharing is a regular part of our lives. She shares what frightens her most to share with me, and I share with her what I most do not want her to know. It is difficult each time. We do it because we have both learned that not sharing what is important is like burying dynamite. It will explode.

Linda has become my spiritual buddy, and I have become hers. Our goal is to grow spiritually, to become whole and inwardly secure. We use our "relationship" to do that. We are not the first people to discover this way of relating, and we will not be the last. Millions are discovering it, and using it. It is the only way that the new male and the new female can relate. It is the only way that they want to. They create this kind of relationship whenever they come together.

This new kind of relationship is as different from other relationships as the new male and the new female are from the old male and the old female. It has its own rules. Sharing what is most frightening to share is one of them.

It also has a name.

Spiritual Partnership

"Almost no one I marry wants to use the traditional ceremony anymore. A few do, but not many."

"What do they want?" I asked, settling into our conversation.

Louie sat back. He had grown handsome in his seventies.

"They want to write their own vows," he said.

"What do they vow?" I asked.

"They tell each other what they are willing to commit to—how they agree to grow together," he said. Then he laughed.

"They all take out the word *obey*. None of them like it."

I had known Louie for twenty years. His silver hair and caring heart were dear to me. Decades as a clergyman had left their imprint, but Louie still liked to rebel as much as he loved to serve. He was doing both now as much as he did when he was in the church.

"So you marry them anyway?" I asked.

"Oh, yes," he said happily. "We talk about the ceremony, we plan it, and then we do it. Each one is different, but the Holy Spirit always comes."

Why do so many people write their own commitments now? A century ago, no one would have thought of that. No one would have married outside of a church, or a tribe.

What has changed?

A century ago there were very few new males and new females. Now there are many, and more are emerging every day. That is what has changed.

The new male and the new female follow their hearts. They are not concerned with what others expect. When they bond, they make their own vows. Those vows are as important to them as the vows that the old male and the old female make, but for a very different reason. The vows of the old female and the old male help them to survive. The old female and the old male come together to create external power. They want lives that are safer and easier. The vows of the new male and the new female help them grow spiritually. The new male and the new female come together to create authentic power. They want lives that are conscious, responsible, and fulfilling.

These differences make new males and new females want to be with each other. What you want most is what you think about and talk about. If you want money more than anything else, you think and talk about money. If you want a good grade more than anything, you think and talk about grades. If you most want to become aware of your feelings, you think and talk about your feelings.

The new male and the new female most want to heal their obsessions, fixations, compulsions, and addictions, so these are the things they talk about. These are not the things that the old male and the old female like to talk about.

When one person talks about baseball, and another talks about tennis, they don't have much in common. The same thing happens when an old male talks with a new female, or an old female talks with a new male. The old male talks about jobs, houses and security. The new female talks about spiritual growth. The old female talks about children and families. The new male talks about spiritual growth.

The new female and the new male want to look at their deepest fears. They like to find out what makes them angry, or frightened. They want to heal all the parts of themselves that are not healthy—like the parts that do not care about other people, and the parts that do not like themselves. They look for ways that they try to control other people, or be controlled by other people. They also look for parts of themselves that feel victimized, and are resentful.

Old males and old females don't do these things. They are not designed to do them. They are designed to protect and provide, and to bear children and raise them. If they are married, they think that their marriage is not working when they get angry, jealous, or frightened. They don't want to rock the boat. The boat is their marriage.

The new female and the new male do what farmers,

millers, and bakers do. They take their grain to the mill, grind it into flour, and bake the flour into bread. The grain is their fear—their anger, shame, jealousy, and sorrow. The mill is their spiritual partnership. The bread is the harmony, co-operation, sharing, and reverence for Life that they create together.

The new female and the new male are partners on a journey of spiritual growth. They want to make the journey. Their love and trust keep them together. Their intuition guides them. They consult with each other. They are friends. They laugh a lot. They are equals.

That is what a spiritual partnership is—a partnership between equals for the purpose of spiritual growth.

What About Marriage?

The groom was handsome. The bride was radiant. A warm, alpine day completed the picture. Snow-covered mountains dominated the distance. Pine trees surrounded the guests. When the ceremony was over, the band played and everyone ate and danced.

Then a very special thing happened. The new husband looked into the eyes of his new wife.

"I trust you," he said, "because I know that you love God more than you love me."

Spiritual partners know that nothing is more important to them than their own spiritual growth. This is what I believe the young man was saying to his bride. If spiritual partners have to choose between their spiritual growth and what their friends expect, or their families expect, they choose spiritual growth. If they have to choose between what their tribe expects, or their church, they choose spiritual growth.

The new husband knew that his wife would always choose her spiritual growth over everything else, including him. As long as he remains committed to his own spiritual growth, they will grow together. That is how spiritual partnership works. Spiritual growth in one partner creates the opportunity for spiritual growth in the other. Then the other has to decide whether to grow or not.

Do you remember John and Carol? Carol was the wife who screamed at her husband, "You are not respecting me!" John was her husband. John didn't know that he wasn't respecting Carol. In Version I, he thought they were just having a misunderstanding. They were, but he wasn't willing to look at it from Carol's point of view. Their marriage dissolved.

Carol was growing. She wasn't willing to live without respect in her marriage. She wasn't willing to submit to another person's will, even her husband's. John wasn't willing to accept these changes in his wife.

In Version II, John struggled to understand Carol, and their marriage was transformed. This is the special power of a spiritual partnership: What your partner challenges you to do when he or she grows spiritually is exactly what you need to do in order to grow spiritually yourself. How could John create harmony, cooperation, sharing, or reverence while he didn't respect his wife? He couldn't. Carol showed him that. She didn't need to talk about authentic power. All she needed to do was to grow spiritually—to "love God more than anything else"—and that is what she did.

John needed to change, but not for Carol. He needed to change for himself. Carol showed him his next step. Spiritual partnership accelerates spiritual growth. In fact, the only way to grow spiritually is through spiritual partnerships.

Until you have the courage to enter into relationships of substance and depth, you cannot develop spiritually. It doesn't matter how long you meditate or pray, or how many intentions you set. Sooner or later you have to apply what you meditated, prayed and intended. That requires other people. When the other people are committed to growing spiritually, too, then you are in a spiritual partnership.

We are all beginning to want spiritual partners, and to create spiritual partnerships. Shallow talk isn't enough anymore. Making money, raising children, and buying houses aren't enough. Only spiritual growth satisfies. That is because we are all becoming new females and new males.

Every spiritual partnership is different. Some look like marriages. Others look like businesses. Others look like baseball teams. Spiritual partners decide what their partnerships look like. They also decide what roles they play in them.

Each spiritual partner sees himself as a soul first, and a personality second. Each is committed to growing spiritually. Each knows that the purpose of spiritual partnership is spiritual growth.

When a marriage, a business, or a baseball team becomes a spiritual partnership, there is no limit to the creativity, love, and spiritual growth that it can produce. Its future is limited only by the choices that the partners make.

Marriages, businesses, and baseball teams that don't become spiritual partnerships don't have a future.

How Long?

"We're getting a divorce," Scott said. "Marilyn is angry, but she knows this has to happen."

I shifted the phone to my other ear.

"We decided this in therapy this morning."

I knew them both, and loved them both. There was nothing to do but listen. Scott was silent for a long time.

"This is tough," he said.

We were both silent.

"This is tough," he said again.

Marilyn's anger was long-term. She supported Scott when he left the bank and became an organic farmer. She supported him when he traveled to farming workshops. She loved him and she loved their children. And she was angry.

They talked about her anger. They went to therapy.

They examined her childhood, her family, and their marriage. They looked at everything. When Scott left on trips, he felt her anger. When he came home, she was still angry.

Years passed. Then came the divorce.

Scott was a new male and Marilyn was a new female. They were not an old male and an old female trying to understand new males and new females. They grew together spiritually, and they intended to grow together spiritually. Their marriage was a spiritual partnership, but it ended anyway. Why did that happen?

It happened because they stopped growing together. Marilyn wasn't changing, and Scott was. They loved each other, but that couldn't keep them together. Scott wanted to be with Marilyn, but he wanted more to be true to himself. Marilyn wanted him to do that, too, but her anger was more important to her.

They did not decide to end their spiritual partnership because things got tough. All spiritual partners get into tough times. Some of those times are intense. They separated because one of them refused to grow and the other moved forward anyway. In the case of Marilyn and Scott, that took decades. This is important to understand. Spiritual partners do not exchange one another lightly. Changing spiritual partners is like changing scenery in the middle of a play. The play goes on.

If you are in the tenth grade and change schools because you don't like your classmates, you will still be in the tenth grade no matter what other school you choose. Spiritual partners know this. They expect to unearth every obstacle to intimacy between them. Those are the things that they want to learn about and change. They have chosen each other to do this with. Their obstacles are not the issue. Healing them is. They are committed to doing that.

There are only two things that can dissolve a spiritual partnership. Marilyn and Scott discovered one of them—spiritual partners cannot grow together if one of them refuses to grow. When that happens, nothing can keep them together. Refusing to grow is different from having a difficult time growing. It is an intention not to grow. Sometimes people know that they are doing this. Sometimes they don't. They think to themselves that they want to grow, but they really don't. The result is always the same—no change. They don't welcome change, no matter what they say. They are stuck, and they prefer staying stuck, even in something as painful as anger.

Being stuck and working to become unstuck is one thing. Being stuck and not really wanting to change is another. The first is what spiritual partners do. The second is what dissolves their partnerships.

For decades Marilyn lived in anger. She loved it more than she loved Scott. She wanted to keep it even more than she wanted to grow spiritually. Eventually, Scott moved on. This was not emotional, or sexual, promiscuity. Promiscuity prevents spiritual partnership. People who are promiscuous use each other. They look at their partners as replaceable. One partner is as good for them as another. Spiritual partners don't do this. They are involved in each other's lives. They are unique to each other. They cannot be exchanged like automobile parts.

This theme has a variation to it. That happens when one

partner decides that she or he does not want to continue growing with the other. She knows that the same issues she has with him will resurface with another partner. She has no illusions about that. Even so, she makes the decision not to grow with her partner, and their partnership dissolves.

The second reason that spiritual partnerships dissolve is very special. One of the partners completes the lessons that he or she formed the partnership to learn. This experience is unmistakable. The issues don't exist anymore. The healing is complete. No scar tissue remains. Not even a trace of it. If the issue was anger, the anger is gone. If the issue was fear, inner wholeness has replaced it. The circumstances that brought the spiritual partnership into being no longer exist. The challenges change. Perceptions change. Behaviors change. Goals change. Everything changes.

When that happens, the spiritual partner who completes his or her lessons no longer requires the same kind of interactions in order to grow spiritually, and the partnership changes accordingly. In other words, spiritual partners stay together as long as they grow together. When they stop growing together, their spiritual partnership dissolves.

A spiritual partnership is a partnership between equals for the purpose of spiritual growth. When spiritual growth stops happening, the partnership stops happening, too.

Psychic Archaeology

After I separated from my fiancée, I missed her terribly. I thought about her every day and every night. I thought of her while I was moving off my ranch and into a nearby town. I thought of her while I was making new friends and learning how to share my life with them. Month after month I thought about her, longed for her, and dreamed about a life with her.

It didn't happen. Our plan was to live apart in order, eventually, to live together. Living apart was not new for us, but not seeing her every other month was. So was not knowing if we would stay engaged. After a year apart, she ended our engagement, and I began a journey that I never could have anticipated.

"I am not engaged anymore," I told my friends.

They looked at me patiently but didn't say anything at first. After a while, I asked them, "What do you think about that?" I was trembling inside. Being engaged had been a big part of my identity.

After a long silence, one of them said gently, "I think you are not feeling this yet."

I didn't believe him at the time, but it was true. As the weeks and months passed, I discovered how true it was. Each day brought more pain, and each night was worse. Have you ever hurt yourself, but you didn't feel the pain until later, when the numbness disappeared and your hurt began to throb? That is what happened to me. I wondered if I could live through it.

Every morning and evening, at every lunch and dinner, every time I thought about us, I asked myself, "How did I create this?" That became my prayer. I wanted to know that more than anything—more even than I wanted to be with my ex-fiancée again. I had felt this same pain before, with other partners. I didn't ever want to feel it again. I didn't think I could survive if I did. I wanted this answer as if my life depended on it, and I think that it did.

I got my answer, but it didn't come all at once.

After several weeks, the thought of "competition" came to me. I called my former fiancée.

"Did your decision have to do with competition?" I asked.

"Yes," she said. A big yes.

At last I had found something to grasp, like a thread in a tapestry. I intended to keep pulling it until the entire mystery unraveled.

I tried to think of times I felt competitive with her. At first, I couldn't remember any. Then memories began to come, first a trickle, and then a flood. I was jolted. I realized that I had been jealous of her friends. I had been jealous of her business. I had been jealous of her charisma, successes, and popularity. I had been jealous of almost everything. This surprised me, but I was even more surprised to discover another layer below my competitiveness.

That was control. I began to remember one time after another when I had tried to control what my fiancée was doing, or feeling, or saying. I criticized the newspaper she read. I tried to dissuade her from watching television. I tried to influence her taste in cars and clothes. I tried to impose my ideas and opinions. Remembering the many ways that I had tried to control her took several more weeks. As I remembered more and more of them, the extent of my attempts to control her became clearer and clearer to me.

Then I discovered beneath my control something else— fear. By now it was winter. Snow covered the trees, and when the wind blew, everything became white with blowing snow. I lay in bed, terrified. I never imagined that I could feel so frightened. I was afraid of the winter. I was afraid of the cold. I was afraid of being alone. I was afraid of everything. "Fear and trembling" took on new meaning. I never knew that I had fear like that in me. When it came, it came like an ocean. *I was afraid to be alive.* I thought this must be the bottom of my painful excavation, but it wasn't.

Beneath my fear I discovered yet another layer: lack of self-worth. This surprised me completely. I had won The American Book Award for *The Dancing Wu Li Masters*. I was praised and celebrated. People wanted to hear what I had to say—but I didn't think that I had anything to say worth listening to. I couldn't imagine people liking me once they got to know who I really was. I felt there must be something wrong with anyone who was attracted to me. I couldn't find anything about me that I appreciated. Until that moment, I had thought so highly of myself. I was shocked.

When I realized that I had no appreciation of myself at all, all of the things that I had discovered suddenly came together. Because I had no self-worth, I did not believe that I had a right to be alive. Because I didn't believe that I had a right to be alive, I was terrified of everything. Because I was terrified of everything, I needed to control everything— and my need was intense because, emotionally, it was a matter of life and death. Because my fiancée was a strong person, my attempts to control her had turned into competition.

My prayer had been answered. All of the pieces of my puzzle came together like a broken mirror magically reassembling itself when a video of the breaking is played backward. I had asked to see how I had created my terrible nightmare. I saw.

This process took months. It took ten years more to integrate it into my life. I started immediately. I went straight to the root of the problem. I didn't work on my fear, control, or competition. I went to work on my lack of self-worth. When I got angry, but didn't speak angrily, I said to myself, "Good work!" If I took two steps forward and slipped back one and a half, I congratulated myself. When I did something that I would have admired in others, I admired it in me. This felt awkward at first. I had no experience in doing these things.

Eventually, I began to change. I discovered how to share myself with friends, to appreciate them, and to let them appreciate me. I am very grateful for all that I learned. My fiancée and I spent only three months together during the two years that we were engaged. We spent our second year living apart, trying to grow back together. I didn't know at the time why we couldn't do that, but I do now.

The distance between her home on one coast and mine on the other reflected the distance inside of me that I needed to keep from her. Maybe it reflected that in her, too. Intimacy is not always comfortable. I thought that we were very intimate because we loved each other so deeply, but I didn't have the courage to be really intimate with her.

I never discussed my deepest fears with her. I never told her how jealous, inadequate, and frightened I felt. She never discussed her fears with me, either. Our engagement did not end because we didn't love each other enough. We loved each other very much, but love isn't enough.

It takes something else to make a spiritual partnership work.

Trust

"I never fell down so many times," Martha said, laughing. "We don't ski in Kansas."

Everyone laughed.

"Each time I got up I remembered a time when I fell down and had to get up again. Sometimes I did it right away, like when I broke my hand. Other times I didn't, like when I got divorced."

No one was laughing now.

"It was like going to graduate school about myself," she continued. "I saw how I am in some situations, and how different I am in others. I also saw how I have responded the same way to some situations most of my life."

Martha was changing as she spoke. Everyone there would always remember her, and her healing adventure. She could have told us about how sore she was, or how tired. Instead, she told us what she learned.

What made the difference between an ordinary ski lesson and a life-changing day? Martha learned to recognize what was important about her experiences, and that had a big payoff for her. She saw that her insights were worth thinking about, and she thought about them. Then she asked for more insights, and more came. By the end of the day, she expected them, and they continued to come. That is why she had so much to tell us.

Most people look to others to tell them what is important. They ask psychologists, priests, and gurus. They read newspapers and books. They watch television and listen to the radio. They find experts.

Martha became her own expert. She didn't have to ask anyone else what her ski lesson could teach her about her divorce and the other painful experiences in her life. She saw for herself, and trusted what she saw.

Do you trust your experiences? When you are having an argument, do you trust that your argument is telling you something important about yourself? When you are fuming, do you trust that your rage is showing you something about yourself that you need to see?

Spiritual partners do. They trust their experiences to show them important things about themselves. That is how they grow spiritually. You can't grow spiritually and stay angry, impatient or jealous. You can't grow spiritually while you are blaming other people for what you are feeling, either.

Spiritual partners look inside themselves—and not at each other—when they get angry, frightened, or sad. They talk about the things that frighten them to speak about. They share what they feel, but they don't blame each other for it. They trust the process.

This is the process: Be aware of everything you are feeling. Look for what your emotions can show you about yourself. Share what you are feeling in a kindly way, like one student sharing an observation with another.

Spiritual partners trust that they are together in order to grow together spiritually. They trust that everything that happens in their partnership helps them do that. This changes the way they see their experiences with each other, the same way that Martha's insights changed the way she saw her ski lesson. She learned something about herself each time she fell. The same thing happens in a spiritual partnership. You learn something about yourself each time you have a disagreement, and you learn more each time you work your way through one. You learn something about yourself each time you withdraw emotionally, and each time you open up again.

The more you learn, the less often you become angry, withdrawn, and frightened. If you try to learn something each time you fall, it won't take you long to keep your balance on skis. If you try to learn something every time you get angry, or sad, or frightened, it won't take you long to keep your balance when you start to feel angry, sad, or frightened.

Some people think that disagreements are not good things, like falls when you are skiing, but spiritual partners don't look at them that way. They see disagreements as ways that friends can learn about themselves, and become better friends.

They look at all of their experiences that way.

PART IV

How It Happens

Children

Spaghetti slipped from Jamie's fork. Tomato sauce covered her mouth. At two and a half, she had not yet mastered the fork. She put it down and ate with her fingers.

I was very happy. My daughter sat across from Linda, and I sat next to Jamie, my first granddaughter. Candlelight softened her tomato-sauce face.

Suddenly Jamie stopped eating and turned toward me. Her face became serious.

"Be gentle," she said, looking directly at me.

Her entire presence had changed. I playfully changed mine to match it, in a grandfatherly way.

"Be gentle with what?" I asked her.

"With yourself!" she replied.

Then she returned to her dinner. Suddenly she was a child playing with spaghetti again.

We sat in silence. I was stunned, and so was everyone else, except Jamie. Self-severity had been a lifelong burden. Being gentle with myself was difficult for me, but how did Jamie know that? She was only two and a half, and, besides, she had only seen me once.

She knew it directly, the same way that you are beginning to know things directly. She used her intuition, although she did not know what that word meant. She just did it. She saw something about me, and she shared it.

When you see something about other people, or about yourself, do you trust what you see the way Jamie did? Knowing something deep inside you is different from knowing something because other people tell you. You know what you know. You might know that it is not appropriate for you to become a doctor, for example, like your father, or go to college because your parents didn't. No one has to explain it to you.

Changing inside is like that. You see things differently, and no one has to explain it to you. Your friends know that you have changed, too. You don't have the same things in common anymore. This happens to everyone. It happens to spiritual partners, too. What happens when spiritual partners change, and they have children?

The old male and the old female think that nothing is worse for a child than becoming separated from its parents. They see themselves—and themselves only—as responsible for the survival of their children. From their point of view, they can't help their children survive as well when they are apart as they can when they are together.

Children

Spiritual partners are also responsible for their children, but they do not experience the same difficulties when they grow apart that the old male and the old female do. Their children do not experience them, either. That is because the children of spiritual partners belong to larger, loving families that do not change. These larger families are also spiritual partnerships.

The children of spiritual partners grow up being cared for by everyone around them. They see more people as aunts and uncles, brothers and sisters, and grandparents than the children of old males and old females. Their families are not only biological. They are extended spiritual families. These extended spiritual families are spiritual partnerships.

When the children of spiritual partners grow up, they naturally care for everyone, too. They see themselves as the aunts and uncles, brothers and sisters, and grandparents of all of the children in their lives. They see everyone as their family.

If you look inside yourself, you may see that you, also, are longing for spiritual partnerships. Millions of people are beginning to feel this longing. Soon, millions more will feel it, too. The new female and the new male create spiritual partnerships naturally. Sometimes they create them like marriages—they share a house together and have children. Sometimes they create them as businesses, or schools, or basketball teams. However they do it, they do it as equals for the purpose of spiritual growth. They become aware of what they are feeling. They learn how to make responsible choices. They strive for harmony, cooperation, sharing, and reverence for Life. Then they naturally look for spiritual partners to cocreate with.

That is how the cycle goes. The inner work comes first, then come spiritual partnerships. A new world is being born this way. When children are born into spiritual partnerships, they grow up in this new world.

They see everyone, including themselves, as souls. They see their aunts and uncles, brothers and sisters, and grandparents as souls. They see their parents that way, too. This is what we are all beginning to do—to see ourselves and others as souls.

This includes our children.

Spiritual Partners

Chris and Leslie made the room warmer just by being there. It was clear that they were in love with each other. They walked through the wide doors of the auditorium hand in hand, as they often walked together.

The room began to quiet. They gracefully took their places behind the long table on the stage. To the right of Chris sat two more couples. To the left of Leslie sat another two. Each person had a microphone and a glass of water. Flowers decorated the table.

"Dear friends," the announcer began. "Welcome to the highlight of our program."

The weekend was coming to an end. The five couples had shared their experiences. Their lectures and workshops had looked at relationship from every angle. Now they came together for the last time.

"We have explored the most difficult terrain in the territory of human experience," the announcer continued, "how to be with one another consciously and lovingly on the one hand, and with integrity on the other. How to be a partner in a deep relationship, and remain true to ourselves at the same time."

Relationship workshops had become popular in the last few years, and this had been one of the best.

"There are no answers that will satisfy everyone," the announcer concluded, "but over the weekend some common themes have emerged. Respect each other. Listen to each other. Say what is difficult to say—do not hide what is important to you. Share in the kindest way that you can.

"This is an opportunity to address your questions to any, or all, of our presenters."

"I have one," said a young man on the left side of the auditorium, raising his hand. An assistant quickly brought him a microphone.

"I know this sounds funny," he started, "but I still don't understand this thing called a 'relationship.' My girlfriend says she is committed to ours, but how can I commit to a 'relationship' when I don't even know what she means, or what ours will be next month."

"You can commit to monogamy," said a woman to the left of Leslie. "In my opinion, you won't have a relationship without that."

"You can commit to staying together no matter what happens. The strength of a relationship lies in the knowledge that you will always be there for each other," said a man to the right of Chris.

Everyone had an answer. At last, Leslie began to speak.

"When I first partnered with Chris, I never realized that *I* was the one who had difficulties with commitment. Try as I might, I could not make a commitment to our relationship, even though we shared so much love." Leslie's voice was clear and firm. It seemed to fill the hall.

"At last, I realized there was only one thing I could commit to with all my heart. That was my own growth—my spiritual growth. I also realized that Chris was the perfect partner for me to do this with, and we have been together ever since.

"It hasn't been easy for either of us, especially at first, but my commitment has never left me. The same is true for Chris."

Chris nodded in agreement.

"That was fifteen years ago," Leslie continued. "Since then we have created a foundation, authored books, and done our best to model spiritual growth in the context of a loving, caring relationship. There are still times when I wonder if we will make it, but so far I have grown through each of those times feeling closer to Chris than I did before.

"My commitment to myself—to my own growth—is the best one I ever made. It is still very much with me. I hold it in my heart every day."

There were more questions and more answers, but Leslie's words hung in the air through all of them. People were still talking about them as they left the auditorium.

Couples like Leslie and Chris have a special quality. They

listen to each other. They laugh together. Even after fifteen years, Leslie and Chris are still excited by what the other has to say. This is the way spiritual partners are when they are growing together. Chris and Leslie were still growing together, and that is what made their relationship so special.

How do you feel when you think about Chris and Leslie? Do you feel comfortable and warm? Is the thought of them pleasing to you? If you are not in a relationship like theirs, would you like to be? Would you like to get to know them?

Would you still feel the same way if Chris were black and Leslie were white? If Leslie were black and Chris were yellow, would the thought of them still be pleasing? Would you still want to get to know them if Chris and Leslie were both women? What if they were both men?

Every spiritual partner is different. One struggles not to see himself as better than other people. Another struggles not to see other people as better than herself. One is learning how to say what he needs. Another is trying not to overpower friends. One needs to learn how to listen. Another needs to learn how to speak.

No matter how different spiritual partners are, they are all learning how to align their personalities with their souls. That is why they are together. They want to create harmony, cooperation, sharing, and reverence for Life.

When you look at spiritual partners, do you see these things? Do you see how difficult their challenges are? Do you admire what they are doing, and appreciate how they are trying to do it?

If you see anything else, your attention has been distracted by something that all of us have.

Earth Suits

Gerald's apron was dusted with white flour. Some of it had gotten on his T-shirt. He wiped his hands on his jeans, smiled at me, and took the money that I handed him.

In the glass case between us were doughnuts and éclairs, some of them covered with chocolate, some with glazed sugar, and some plain. These and ice cream were all that the small bakery sold. In the afternoon, students came after school, and, in the morning, older people drank coffee in vinyl booths and read newspapers.

I came to this bakery often to ship packages, a service Gerald also provided. Over the years, we had come to recognize each other. During that time, Gerald's appearance never changed. He always had long brown hair and wore jeans, a T-shirt, and an apron.

One day I heard a knock on my door. It was Gerald, but his appearance had changed completely. He was wearing a fashionable suit, and his hair was short. He looked like a prosperous businessman. As I admired his new appearance, he handed me his card.

"I came to tell you about my new business," he said, with warmth and authority. "I am an investment broker. This is my new office," he continued, pointing to the address on the card. "If I can help you with your investments, please let me know." He appeared to be a perfect person to discuss investments with. If I had not known him as he was at the bakery, I would not have suspected that he had ever done anything except help people become wealthy through investing their money.

The baker, the modest young man in jeans and an apron, and the investment broker, the prosperous young man in the business suit, were both Gerald. He had begun a new life, and his clothing had changed accordingly. I knew that his experiences would change dramatically, too, and I marveled to realize that he was still the same young man.

I am happy that I knew Gerald when he owned a bakery, and later when he became an investment broker. If I had known him only when he was a baker, or only when he sold investments, I might not have appreciated how diverse his experiences were. I might have thought of him as a baker, or an investment broker, and never realized that he was both, and more.

Gerald changed his clothing when he wanted to have different experiences. Souls do that, too. Sometimes they are female. Others times they are male. Those times are lifetimes. Sometimes they are black. Other times they are white, yellow, or brown. Sometimes they have families, and sometimes they organize political movements. Changing clothes is not new to souls. Your soul has done it often. It has also had the many experiences that come with different kinds of clothing.

When you look at yourself as a black male, or a white female, you are only seeing some clothes. This is how most people see themselves. They think of themselves as men, women, black, yellow, fathers or mothers, or any of the many ways that souls can dress. This is a five-sensory perception. When you begin to know that you are more than a body with some thoughts and feelings, you are becoming multisensory. Then you look at yourself as a soul, and not just as a brown female, or white male. You see all of those things—your race, sex, height, hair color, culture—as clothes that your soul is wearing.

These are the clothes that your soul chose when it created you. You are not your clothes. You are your soul. What you can see with your five senses are not your friends. They are only the clothes that your friends are wearing. Your friends are souls, too. Her black body, or his yellow body, is clothing. Do you like or dislike someone because of the clothes that he or she is wearing?

That is what you do when you do not like someone because of the color of his skin, or because she is a female, or Catholic, or Vietnamese, or an athlete, or poor, or wealthy, or any of the ways that souls choose to dress. A yellow, Thai, Buddhist mother is a suit. A white, German, Jewish father is also a suit. So is a brown, Brazilian, Catholic rancher. They are Earth suits.

Once you make a friend, it doesn't matter what clothes

he or she wears. A friend is a friend. This is how souls see souls. They are friends. The clothes that they wear are not important, just like the clothes that Gerald wore when he stopped being a baker and became an investment broker were not important. He was still Gerald. He wanted to have some new experiences, so he put on some new clothes.

Your soul has done that many times. You have been a mother and a father, a city dweller and a nomad. You have been strong and weak. You have been quick-witted and slow. You have lived violent lives and peaceful lives. You have been kind and you have been cruel. You have been black, white, yellow and red.

Each of these was an Earth suit, like the one that you are wearing now. Each was carefully chosen by your soul. It wouldn't have worked for Gerald to wear a business suit while he was baking pastry, or to wear T-shirts while he was selling investments. Souls see one another as souls who are wearing different Earth suits the same way that I saw Gerald wearing the clothing of a baker at one time, and the clothing of a businessperson the next.

Souls are always happy to see each other again. They are happy to see what clothing each is wearing also, but that is not important to them. Being together is important to them. Learning how to create harmony, cooperation, sharing, and reverence for Life together is important to them.

As you become multisensory, you begin to see your friends that way, too. You even begin to see your enemies that way. This is very different from the way that most people look at their friends and enemies.

It is also the beginning of some very exciting things.

Active Kindness

No one knows where the lightning struck. By the time crews could reach the area, it was surrounded by hundreds of charred acres. If it were not for the valiant effort of the firefighters, perhaps thousands would have burned. What was once a great forest was now a wasteland. Blackened trunks emerged from a moonscape of lifeless soil. It would be generations before the shade returned. In the meantime, the sun shone relentlessly through the thinning smoke. The smell of charcoal filled the air, and the ground was still hot.

Unnoticed through all of this were the tiny seeds that lay scattered on the ashen soil. In them another forest lay waiting, making itself ready to replace the old. Thousands of older trees had given themselves to the fire. Thousands more were now ready to grow. In slow motion, so slow that none of us can see it, a picture is unfolding. All that we notice is the fire. It is awesome. It cannot be overlooked. Roaring flames leaping a hundred feet into the air. Billows of dense, gray smoke float over thousands of acres, obscuring the horizon. It is over and done with in a few days.

The picture that we cannot see is unfolding much more slowly. The fire is a part of that picture, but it is not all of it. To see the rest we would have to live for hundreds of years. We would have to see the fire before this one. No trace of that fire remained by the time the lightning struck again. An ocean of green stretched from ridge to ridge. That ocean grew out of blackened trunks just as a new ocean of green will now grow. Without the fire, the seeds would not have burst forth. Without the seeds, new trees would not grow. Without new trees, the forest would decay.

Is the forest that is waiting to grow different from the forest that just burned? They are the same. They are all the same forest—the trees that burned and the trees that will grow because of the fire, and the trees that grew because of fires that no one can remember.

Today we try to stop forest fires because people have homes in forests, and because cutting trees is a big business. Fires do not threaten the forests. The forests need fires, and they happen naturally. Some people say that lightning strikes are accidents. If you look at all of nature, the lightning strikes don't look that way. From the point of view of nature, everything happens at just the right time.

If you look carefully, the rain falling on dry ground is just what the plants need to grow. The plants and the rain are parts of the same picture. If you look only at the plants, or you look only at the rain, you don't see the whole picture. That is like seeing only the fire. Even one animal eating another is part of a larger picture.

Nature always provides what is needed when it is needed. Always providing what is needed when it is needed is active kindness. We don't think of nature as being kind, but it is. If we see the whole picture, we can see that nature is always kind. Sometimes we don't think of the Universe as being kind, either, but it is. If we see only a selfish person, or someone suffering, we see only part of a larger picture. If we could see the whole picture, we would be amazed at how compassionate the Universe is.

We can't ever see the whole picture, but one thing is certain—it contains other people. One other thing is certain. It also contains us. So the first step in seeing more of the picture is to start seeing ourselves and others clearly. That is where active kindness begins.

People who have hurt a lot in their lives are often kind. They know what it is to suffer, and they don't want to cause anyone else to suffer. They don't harm Life, and so we say that they are kind. Active kindness is more than this. Active kindness takes strength and clarity. Sometimes it requires speaking when it is difficult to speak. Sometimes it requires not speaking when you want to. Sometimes it means being brave enough to act, and at other times it means being brave enough not to act.

Active kindness is being appropriate. That is how souls relate to souls. They see more than Earth suits. Do you think that you do not deserve to be loved? That is your

Earth suit talking. If you see only from that perspective, you can never be appropriate. Your heart will always tell you that you deserve to love and to be loved, that you are beautiful, and that you have a right to be on this Earth.

Do you think that you are more important than other people? If you see only from that perspective, you can never be appropriate, either. Your heart will always tell you that everyone is important. It will tell you that no one is more important than you, and that no one is less important than you, either. When you see only Earth suits, you see only a small part of a larger picture. When you see yourself and others as great souls in the Earth school, you see a lot more of it.

Then you can act the way that you soul wants to act, and say what your soul wants to say. Then what you say and do will always be appropriate. It will always be just what is needed, just when it is needed. That is active kindness.

It is also authentic power.

Reaching Out

The two skaters moved as one. One was male, the other female. One wore black, the other white. The blades of their skates flashed in the lights that followed them over the ice. Music filled the arena. Where it went, they went. After a while, I couldn't tell whether the music was moving them, or they were making the music when they moved. The music, lights, ice, skaters, and all of us merged.

I could feel their danger. Every movement was intricate. Each of them required perfect timing. Each would have been difficult on a dance floor. The skaters performed them all at high speed, first with one skater moving backward, then the other, then both backward, then both forward.

As they came toward my part of the arena again, they

separated. She moved to her right, and he to his left. The tempo of the music rose toward a crescendo. Suddenly they veered toward each other, very fast. Her arms reached out to him, and he grasped them. In an instant her body lifted off the ice. With her legs perfectly together, she became a white crane taking flight before our eyes. High over her partner's head she soared, held tightly in his strong hands.

Her skates returned to the ice as gracefully as they left it. Still perfectly with the music, they were moving forward again, cheek to cheek, toward the cheering crowd. We were dazzled by their boldness and strength, their ingenuity and creativity, and their courage and skill. We skated with them, in our own ways. If they had fallen, we would have fallen, too, and felt their pain.

They worked together perfectly. Their strengths blended into a powerful performance that neither could have accomplished alone. All of their times apart on the ice were in preparation for their times together. That is when their talents combined in special ways. They were both virtuoso skaters. Either could have performed alone. They chose to perform together, and together they created something that no solo skater could accomplish.

It is one thing to see timing and perfection in an individual, like a great diver, or gymnast. It is another to see individuals combine their talents. That lifts the activity to another level. As we begin to see ourselves as souls, we begin to move from being solo performers to individuals in partnership with each other. This happens naturally and easily. We like the feeling of working together. We like giving our gifts, and we like others receiving them. We also like receiving the gifts of others. Like the skaters, we can do things together that we cannot do alone. Our strengths combine in ways that give us opportunities that we would not have otherwise.

There is no way that the skater who became a white crane could have flown without her partner to lift her, and no way that he could have used his strength and balance so beautifully without her to lift. She trusted him completely. The ice was as hard as concrete. She sailed seven feet above it, vulnerable and defenseless if he should stumble. He was committed to her completely. Together, they awed us as neither could have done separately. It was not only their skill, strength, and creativity that kept us on the edges of our seats. It was their teamwork and their trust in each other.

Souls are like that, too. They reach out for one another like the grass reaches for the sky, and the sky reaches back for the grass. All of nature does this, if you look for it. Flowers reach for the sun, and the sun reaches back to the flowers. The shore reaches for the sea, and the sea reaches for the shore. Souls do not come together in order to get things done, like make money, raise a family, or create a business. They come together because that is their nature.

They delight in each other. They give one another the opportunities that each of them requires in order to reach his or her fullest potential, as the young skaters gave each other opportunities to reach their fullest potential.

As you become aware of yourself as a soul, people become more interesting to you. You like being with them, and you like getting to know them. You like letting them get to know you. If you only think of yourself as your Earth suit, this doesn't always happen. If you only see the Earth suits of the souls around you, it doesn't always happen, either. When you see yourself as a soul, and you see other people as souls, it always happens. This doesn't mean that you tell everyone everything about you all of the time. It means that you are always open to others, and appreciate them.

The shore and the sea are always combining in new ways. Even if you watched them every day of your life, not one of their moments together would be like any other. That is the way that it is with souls, too. No two of their moments together are the same. They delight in their endless creativity.

As we become aware of ourselves as souls, we do the same thing.

Inner Richness

Casper struggled up the ridge. Soft dirt crumbled under his feet, tiring him. Sweat poured from his forehead and trickled down his face. It stung when it reached his eyes. His arms were covered with sweat, too, and his shirt was wet with it. He gasped for breath when he reached the top, and wiped his forehead with a dirty piece of cloth.

The sun was high. He had been climbing ridges since it first appeared. There was no shade. Manzanita branches interlocked to make barriers around him wherever he looked. Only a deer could move through this thick growth, but Casper had managed to do it. Now hundreds of feet more of it greeted him as he came to the top of the ridge and looked beyond it toward the trees in the distance below him.

If it weren't for the manzanita, he could be in the trees in no time. He would reach them, somehow. As he paused to catch his breath, the sound of running water, barely audible, came to him on the breeze. He cupped his hands behind his ears. Yes, it was water, not the wind. The sound was coming from the trees. There was water there, and shade, too. More than that, there was something that had been pulling Casper for years. Now it was pulling him down a gully toward trees that grew along a stream at the bottom.

Behind him, at the bottom of the ridge that he had just climbed, a mule grazed. Beside it were packs that carried Casper's food, tools, and clothing. He thought of going back to get them, then looked again toward the trees. He decided to go for the trees, and get the supplies later. No matter where he looked, no matter where he went, it was work. He had worked and sweated for years, exploring unknown valleys and streams, lakes and basins in his quest. The quest never stopped. It always pulled him forward.

As he approached the trees, the sound of water became louder, and the gully sides became steeper. The stream, clear and fresh, rushed downward over a rock bed twenty feet below him. He slid down the steep bank and came to a stop beside it. Dropping to his knees, he put his head into the cool, sweet water and splashed it over his shoulders. Then he lay back and rested for the first time that morning.

"This is the place," he said to himself. "This is the place." He had said that many times before, and each time it had not been the place. Now the old feeling came to him again, and he knew that, again, he would dig.

It took the rest of the day to get back to the mule and return with his supplies. The next day he began to dig. He continued digging for three weeks. By the beginning of the fourth week, he had excavated a large hole in the side of the steep embankment. It was big enough for Casper to enter standing. It extended back into the cool earth so far that Casper needed his lantern to continue digging. Loose rock and soil gathered in piles on either side of him, waiting to be taken, a sackful at a time, out of the hole.

His arms were weary. His body ached. "It's got to be here," he said out loud. "I know it's here. I know it." All the years of digging weighed down on him now. He fought fatigue. He struggled to focus. "I will find it," he repeated yet again, perhaps for the thousandth time. "I will not stop until I find it."

As his pick went into the rock in front of him, he felt something different. The rock yielded! He swung again, and again his pick entered soft rock. He moved the lantern closer and brought some of the rock to it. It glowed in the soft light, the way that only gold can glow. Casper's search had come to an end.

In that moment, Casper became a wealthy man. His struggles would not end, but they would never be the same again. Now he had wealth at his service. He had freedom. He had the ability to create as he chose. His life had changed. This moment did not come quickly. It took years of effort to arrive at it. It took faith and hard work. It took courage and strength.

Inner richness is like that. It does not lie on the surface, waiting to be picked up. It doesn't sparkle in the sun, drawing you to it. Casper found the mother lode, thick veins of gold running through protective rocks. Inner richness also lies deep inside, but not inside the Earth. It lies deep inside you. If you look outside, you will never find it. When you look inside, you will always find it, if you are determined enough, like Casper. Casper dug in a lot of places before he found what he was looking for. It was hard work, but he kept at it.

How much digging do you do in your life? When something unpleasant happens, do you look inside to see what you can learn? When a tragedy happens, like the death of a child, do you try to see what this painful experience means? Digging in your life means looking for what you can learn about yourself when you are feeling angry, sad, or frightened. If you don't look for what you can learn about yourself when you feel these things, you aren't digging. If you don't dig, you won't find the gold.

Everything—even things that are painful—happens for a reason. That reason is to help you grow spiritually. When you see that, you hit pay dirt. Until you find it, you will always be disappointed when you don't get what you want, and happy only when you do. When you find the gold, everything in your life becomes a gift that is designed especially for you. Everything in everyone else's life is a gift that is designed especially for them. Once you find inner richness, no one can take it from you. It is yours forever.

Casper knew that he would find what he was looking for. He kept looking because he believed that it was there.

That is how you find your inner richness, too.

Perfect Trust

I leaned into the wind. Snow was blowing from the summit. I tried to see the top of Misery Hill, but I couldn't. I looked back. To my surprise, Avalanche Gulch was clear. I could see five thousand feet straight down the snow-filled ravine. As if by magic, only the route that I had taken up was clear. Everything else was hidden in turbulent, swirling gray.

I would be on the summit in an hour. Then the sky turned a very dark and forbidding blue. Even the light place in the clouds where the sun had been disappeared. The snow flew horizontally, and became thicker. I knew the head wall of glacier dropped a hundred feet to the ice below on the right side of the ridge I was climbing. On the left, rock chutes dropped fifty feet into Avalanche Gulch. In a whiteout, I wouldn't be able to see either.

I turned once more into the snow. Then I started down. I had visited the summit many times. This time I would not. I could see a magnificent pinnacle below me. I knew it well. I had reached thirteen thousand feet. I walked slowly now, even though the wind was at my back. I loved every part of this mountain. I savored every moment on it. It had been my home, my majestic neighbor, and my teacher. Now I prayed that I would find my way down it one more time.

When I had descended a thousand feet, sunlight broke through the clouds. The summit remained hidden in the ferocious storm above me. Two climbers slowly made their way upward, headed where I had been. I wished them well. I could see a city sparkling in the sunlight fifty miles away. My climb started at two in the morning. Now it was nine. I was ready to return to Linda and our warm house a mile and a half below.

Patches of sunlight floated over the snow, changing it from gray to sparkling white to gray again. By the time I reached the trees, clouds covered the entire sky again. It rained all the way home, beating against the windshield while I maneuvered through the last curves in the long road. As I sat in front of the fire, happy to be warm and dry, it seemed to me that it was raining all over the world.

Have you ever felt that way? Have you ever felt that the sun would never shine again, even though you knew that it would? How did you know that it would? No one can prove it, but you know that it will, anyway. You know that it is shining on people somewhere. You don't waste your time wondering about that, even though you can't see it, and no one can demonstrate it.

While I was climbing, the storm around me was all that I could see. I was worried about getting down, but I wasn't worried about not seeing the sun again if I did. I never doubted that I would.

That is perfect trust. When you know something so well that you never doubt it, even though no one can prove it, that is perfect trust. No one has to convince you, and you don't need to convince anyone else. No one has to prove to you that you are breathing. You know that you are.

When you see yourself as a soul, no one has to convince you that you are a soul. Being a soul is even more real than breathing to you because someday you will stop breathing, but you will never stop being a soul. It is even more real than the sun because someday the sun will disappear, but you soul won't. Nothing that you can see, hear, smell, taste, or touch lasts forever.

Your soul does. It sees more than the five senses can see. It sees everything that happens in your life as a way for you to learn important things about yourself. When you see yourself as a soul, you see that, too. You don't have to be convinced. You don't waste your time wondering about it. You know it the way I knew the sun would shine again after the storm.

When you see everything that happens in your life as a way for you to learn important things about yourself, you start to look more closely at the things that happen in your life. The more you do, the more you learn about yourself. The more you learn about yourself, the more you can change the things that happen. After a while, you are happy for everything that happens, even things that are unpleasant.

Then everything that happens is a special gift. You don't have to prove that to anyone, and no one has to prove it to you. It is, and you know it. You don't doubt it, and nothing can make you doubt it.

That is perfect trust.

Love

Once upon a time there was a microbe named Michael. He had a lot of friends. Some of them were more special to him than others, but all of them were microbes. They lived in the bark of a giant tree, although none of them knew that. To them, the entire world was a world of microbes and the kinds of things that microbes see every day and every night. Microbes are tiny compared to even the smallest piece of bark. They are so tiny that they cannot even imagine what bark is, much less trees.

Life for a microbe is a miraculous mystery. No one knows how it started, and no one knows how or when it will end. One day a microbe is here, and the next day it is not. Everyone has their ideas about this, but no one knows for sure how it happens. If you took a step back from the world of microbes, you would see another world. This is the world of bugs. One of those bugs is named Benny. Benny lives on the bark, and Michael lives on Benny. Benny doesn't know about Michael, and Michael doesn't know abut Benny, but they both live in the same tree.

The tree is named Terry. Terry is huge compared to you and me, and even larger compared to a bug or a microbe. She has thousands of leaves, hundreds of branches, and scores of roots. Some of them are as big as small trees. All of them are visited by bugs like Benny and microbes like Michael.

Terry is part of a forest. The forest doesn't have a name, but for convenience, we can call it Frank, and pretend that it is a male forest. Frank has millions of trees and seedlings, along with countless bushes, plants, and flowers. He also has animals and birds. All of them, too, have microbes and bugs like Michael and Benny and their friends. When you put all of this together, you can see how big the forest is compared to anything that lives in it, but that is just the beginning.

Frank is one of thousands of forests, and all of them are part of a larger picture. The larger picture has more than just more forests. It has oceans. It has deserts. It has mountains and prairies. All of these have microbes and bugs, too. (Yes, even the ocean has its own kind of bugs, and its own kind of microbes.) No matter how big the picture gets, it's the same story. There are little parts of the picture and big parts of the picture. There are also in-between parts of the picture, but it is all the same picture. So far, we all know about this picture. It is the Earth. Aboriginal people call it Mother Earth, and they see all of us and everything on it as her children. This is a beautiful picture that everyone likes very much, but there is more.

Mother Earth has lots of friends. There are other planets and there are stars. There are also moons. Benny and Michael have no idea about these things. They don't even know about trees, but they are still part of this picture, and the picture never stops getting bigger. All of the stars—like the sun—and the planets—like Mother Earth—are part of a galaxy. A galaxy is a family with millions of stars and planets. Suppose that we call our galaxy Gail. You may think that Gail is pretty big, but from her point of view, she is just one of the girls. When she looks around, she sees *millions of galaxies.* Gail sees as many galaxies in the sky as we see stars. Now the picture is really getting big, even from our point of view, much less Michael's and Benny's.

So far we have been talking about how the picture gets bigger and bigger. It also gets smaller and smaller, if you want to look at it that way. Michael doesn't know it, but he is made up of molecules, such as Mary. Mary is made up of atoms, such as Amy, and Amy is made of subatomic particles like Sarah and Sam. The picture gets even smaller, too, but you can already see what is happening. This picture is really big and it is really small at the same time, but no matter how you look at it, it is the same picture.

Now here's the point: Every part of the picture needs every other part. Even the mountains, which are millions of years old, need the microbes, which don't live very long. Even the galaxies, which have hundreds of millions of stars and planets, need the atoms and the molecules. No part of the picture can get along without any other part of the picture.

You are part of the picture. You may think that the picture can get along without you because it was here before you were born and it will be here after you die. That is true, but it still can't get along without you. It can't get along without anything that is in it, ever. When you look at yourself as your Earth suit, it seems that the picture can get along without you when you die. When you see yourself as a soul, you see that you are always part of the picture. You always need everything in the picture, and everything in the picture always needs you.

That is love. When you see that you and Michael, Benny, Frank, Mother Earth, Gail, and everything else that you can see and that you can't see are part of the same picture, your life lights up with love. Everything becomes important to you, like friends that you are grateful for. The trees become important, and the bugs, and the oceans and other people. You are all in the same picture together. You are all important parts of the picture.

This is what you see when you see the way that your soul sees. Your Earth suit sees only the parts. Your soul sees the picture. When it looks at itself, it sees the picture. When it looks at other people, it sees the picture. Wherever it looks, it sees the picture.

More and more people are beginning to see the picture. That is multisensory perception. More and more people are choosing harmony, cooperation, sharing, and reverence for Life, even when choosing them is difficult. That is creating authentic power.

Eventually, we will all choose to create authentic power.

This situation is very new, indeed.

It is the beginning of something that has never happened before.

Universal Humans

Olive trees grew behind low stone walls on either side of the dirt road, no different from those that grew in the same fields thousands of years ago. Palestine had changed since those days, and yet it had not changed at all. The adobe houses, pottery water jars, and donkeys were all the same. Generations of brutal warfare could not change that. Bulldozed houses and army patrols, air strikes and artillery bombardments could not change it. International terrorism and media exploitation could not change it. The land was ancient, and so were the roots that sank into it, Jewish and Arabic, Palestinian and Israeli.

Leah's stomach was in knots. How could she tell them? What could she say that would not make them feel their trust had been betrayed? To them, she was an American.

They looked upon her as a friend from afar, an acknowledgment from the rest of the world of Palestinian suffering, and the injustice of it. She was one of the group. Again and again the group had traveled to the Holy Land to meet with these families, to witness their misery, and to offer them an open heart. They had come to love her, and she had come to love them. Now there was only one thing left for her to tell them—she was Jewish.

They were aghast. Angry words flew, and some tears fell. It took most of the afternoon and the night before a new quietness began to form. She was Jewish, and they loved her. They were Palestinian, and she loved them. Now what? A new life had begun for Leah and for the village. She returned to New York with a vision that she could never have imagined two weeks earlier—she would return to Palestine not only as a Jew, but in the company of a group of Jews! They would go to the same places, meet the same friends, and share the same meals—as Jews.

The boldness of the vision startled her. For years she had lived in fear for her life if she should be discovered as a Jew. Now she would wear her Judaism around her heart as a holy cloth, and share it with the families she had come to love—in Palestine.

She gathered a small group of Jews and made preparations for a return trip. They prayed together. They decided what they would do. They would listen. Everywhere they went, they would listen. They would listen with open hearts. They would listen without judgment. They called their method compassionate listening.

They were frightened at first. They entered Hebron,

known for its terrible violence between Palestinian youth and Israeli soldiers, and they listened. They went from village to village, and from settlement to settlement, meeting all the people who had come to love Leah, and they listened. After two weeks, their fear was gone. Their pilgrimage became a journey from one loving family to another. Some were Israeli, and some were Palestinian.

At one Israeli settlement on the West Bank of the Jordan River, they walked each morning to a neighboring Palestinian village. On the first morning, they walked alone. On the second, a few youths from the settlement came with them—without their weapons. It was a very brave thing for them to do, but they did it, anyway. They were greeted with joyous disbelief when they arrived. Tears fell when it came time to leave. On the third day, nineteen people from the settlement, including adults, came with them.

Everyone in the village stopped working. The mayor wanted to slaughter a lamb for a celebration and a feast. There was not enough time for that, so they celebrated together in the best ways that they could. They celebrated seeing each other for the first time without weapons and without rocks. They celebrated looking into each other's eyes. They celebrated what they saw.

"There was so much longing to connect," Leah told me, "but no one knew how to do it. We provided a vehicle. Before we came, there was no way for Israelis, even liberals, to meet their Arab neighbors. There was no way for Arabs to meet their Israeli neighbors, either."

As Leah's small group left Israel a month later, Palestinians in villages all over the West Bank were still marveling

that Jews had been in their houses, and Israelis in their set-
tlements were still marveling that they had shared food and
talk in the houses of their Palestinian neighbors. Only old
people had memories of such a thing.

Now they all had new memories.

"Everyone knows that God promised us the land of Israel," said a young rabbi who was on the trip. "What He
didn't say was that He promised it to someone else, too.
Now we have to learn to live together."

We are all learning the same thing. Arabs are learning it
about Jews, white people are learning it about black people, Asians are learning it about Europeans, men are learning it about women, and adults are learning it about
children. Everybody is learning it about everybody. We are
learning that life together is a celebration. Grief is the same
in everyone. So is joy. No one's life is easy in the Earth
school. What is more worthy of our precious lives than to
love each other? The harder that is to do, the more it is
worth the effort.

When we see each other as souls wearing Earth suits,
loving each other becomes easier. Then none of the things
that seem important to us when we think that we are our
Earth suits seem important anymore. Being yellow, black,
brown or white doesn't seem important. Neither does being French, or Indian, or American. Being rich or poor,
young or old, or female or male doesn't seem important,
either. Nothing seems important except that we are souls
together in the Earth school.

When one of us hurts, that is a sorrow for everyone. When
one of us is happy, that is a joy to everyone. We are all living

in the same promised land. It belongs to each of us, and we belong to it. That is the Universe. There is no other land. Palestine is part of the Universe. Israel is part of the Universe. Muslims, Jews, men, women, Christians, Hindus, intellectuals and athletes are part of the Universe. Horses, cows, trees, birds, leopards, and flowers are part of the Universe, too. The Earth is part of the Universe.

The things that we can't see with our five senses are also part of the Universe. There is a lot that we can't see with our five senses, but we are beginning to become aware of some of it as we become multisensory. We have nonphysical guides. They are part of the Universe. We have nonphysical Teachers. They are part of the Universe, too. Everything is part of the Universe.

Leah first came to Palestine as an American. She discovered that she loved some people there. Then she realized that she needed to share with them the thing that she thought most kept them apart—that she was Jewish. When she did that, she discovered how deep their love really was. She was still an American and still a Jew, but something was very different. Those things weren't as important to her anymore as the people that she loved. They weren't as important anymore to the people who loved her, either.

The Palestinian Arabs and the American Jews became a family together. That was important to them. The family grew to include Israeli Jews, too. That family is still growing. It is part of a family that is growing in you and growing in me. More and more of us are discovering that we want the same thing now, and we are beginning to create it. That is a family that includes *everyone* and *everything*.

Universal Humans

We are becoming Universal Humans. We are beginning to see everyone and everything as part of our family—a Universal Family. Being in a family is not always easy. This is a family that no one can leave. As we become Universal Humans, we don't want to leave it. We want to be together, and to create things together—like harmony, cooperation, sharing, and reverence for Life. We want to share our love, just as Leah's group and the Palestinians and the Israelis that they visited did.

The idea of being in the same family with everyone and everything is very satisfying, and it makes us feel good. That is because, as we learn how to do it, we are becoming something that we could never have dreamed.

Elegant Spirits

Little Hawk sat alone on the grassy knoll. That was not his real name, but that is what everyone called him. Every day he came to the same knoll and sat silently, looking toward the sky. Every day—almost— a red tail hawk flew above him. Sometimes it was already there when Little Hawk arrived. Sometimes it appeared after he came, at first just a speck in the clear sky. Sometimes other hawks came, and, in the winter, eagles came, too. Little Hawk watched them all.

This day the grass on the knoll was yellow, leaves were dropping, and an August breeze caressed him. Above Little Hawk, three red tail hawks circled, riding the currents of air that rose from the knoll. They were lower than usual, and it seemed to Little Hawk that he could see every feather on the elegant birds. The air currents were invisible to Little Hawk, but the birds rode them as skillfully as deer leaping over a fallen tree, or fish swimming up a river.

How do they do that? he wondered.

As one of the hawks—the one that came almost every day—hovered above him, Little Hawk saw its tail feathers move ever so slightly. First one on the left, then one in the middle, then one on the left again, shifted position. The more Little Hawk watched, the more he could see how these movements kept the hawk just where it wanted to be as the air moved around it.

"The hawk is dancing with the wind!" he exclaimed.

At that moment, the hawk moved its wings slightly. It didn't flap them. It just moved them a little bit. At once it began to circle upward. Little Hawk watched as it grew smaller and smaller. When it was very high in the sky, two more hawks joined it, and they flew away together.

Little Hawk thought about what he had seen for a long time. He thought about it all fall and winter. He was still thinking about it in the spring. Something very big was happening inside him. Little Hawk was learning something about his own life from the hawk—how to ride the wind.

Hawks are masters at flying. They can glide. They can climb and dive. They can land in trees. They are masters of their wing feathers and their tail feathers, but they are not masters of the wind.

The wind goes where it wants. Sometimes the wind blows from the north and sometimes from the south. Sometimes it comes from the east and sometimes from the west. Sometimes it flies straight up, and sometimes it roars straight down. It can disappear and reappear from nowhere.

No matter how it blows, hawks love to fly. They move

with the wind, but not like leaves in the autumn breeze. Leaves in the wind go where the wind goes, and sometimes that happens to hawks, too. Sometimes it doesn't. The journey of a leaf depends only on the wind. Hawks have wills of their own.

The journey of a hawk depends on both the hawk and the wind. Sometimes the wind takes the hawk where it wants to go, and sometimes it doesn't. When it doesn't, the hawk doesn't mind. Either way, hawks are masters at flying, always in control of their wing feathers and tail feathers.

Elegant spirits do this, too. Their wing feathers and tail feathers are what they think, say, and do. They always think, say, and do things to create harmony, cooperation, sharing, and reverence for Life. No matter what comes up, that is what they do. They are in control of what they think, say and do, even though they are not in control of what comes up in their lives. Sometimes unpleasant things come up. Other times happy things come up. Either way, they ride the wind. They do the best they can, and then they let the wind take them where they need to go.

The wind is your life. It is all the things that happen between the time that you are born and the time that you go home. Elegant spirits don't know what will come up next, the same way that hawks don't know which way the wind will blow next. This doesn't bother them because they don't try to control their lives any more than hawks try to control the wind.

The hawk that hovered above Little Hawk did not try to control the wind. It controlled only itself. Elegant spirits control only themselves, too. They do not try to control others. They don't have hidden agendas. They don't think, say, or do things to manipulate other people. They do their best, but they aren't attached to what happens after that. Like the hawks, they do the best that they can, then they ride the wind.

The hawk that hovered above Little Hawk never stopped using its wing feathers and its tail feathers. Elegant spirits never stop using their intentions. Their intentions are to create harmony, cooperation, sharing, and reverence for Life. They set them, do their best, and then say, "Thy will be done." That is how they ride the wind. They do not fight their lives. They use them to soar.

What Little Hawk learned from the hawk changed his life. From that time on, he began to soar, too.

Have you soared in your life yet? If not, you may be surprised. When you do, you will discover that the wind—your life—is not taking you just anywhere.

Sacred Tasks

Abdul's journey began long before he could remember. His father taught him about the desert. His grandfather taught his father. His great-grandfather taught his grandfather. The desert was all that Abdul knew—the searing sun, the scorching sand, and the freezing nights. Barren dunes stretched to the horizon in every direction. Nothing grew. There was no shade during the day, and no warm place at night. This wild, desolate land swung between the extremes of ice and fire day after day, night after night.

Water was the difference between life and death in the desert. Abdul knew where to find it. He knew where to dig. He knew every damp piece of sand and every oasis.

The desert was Abdul's life. He was born there, and he

expected to die there. Only a few had seen the edge of the desert, where endless sand meets endless water. Abdul was one of them. It was the most dangerous journey that young Abdul had made. Now he was on one even more dangerous.

An oasis shimmered in the distance. It appeared close, but Abdul knew that it was three hours away. He would rest there for a day and sleep there for a night. He needed his strength. Beyond that meager place lay uncharted territory. No one could help him now, and he knew it.

The oasis was even smaller than it had appeared. A few palms grew by a small spring. He hobbled his camels and unstrapped their heavy loads. Tomorrow they would be heavier. He would take all the water they could carry, and then pray. No one—not even the old men—could tell him if there was a next oasis. He had reached the edge of the known. The idea came to him again that his life until now had been a preparation for this trip.

There was a next oasis, but it took a very long time to reach it. Abdul was too weak to show his excitement. He fell from the camel and crawled to a small spring where clear, sweet water bubbled from the sand. Ever so slowly—one drop at a time—he drank the precious liquid. He wanted to rest there for days, but he could not. His food, now, was running low.

The next oasis was closer and bigger. Sweet fruit grew on strange trees. He drank and ate, and ate and drank. The next day, he started out again. It wasn't long before he reached another oasis. The following day he discovered yet another, and then another, and then another. The oases were getting closer together. Abdul was feeling different, too. The sun wasn't quite as hot, and the nights weren't as cold.

Abdul barely noticed when the sand turned to soil. He did notice when the first bushes appeared. They were unlike anything he had seen. They weren't trees—but what were they? A little farther, Abdul saw more grass than he had seen in his entire life. Instead of the small patches that grew in oases, large expanses spread before him. Day by day as he traveled the expanses became greener and thicker.

The camels weren't used to this landscape. They missed the burning sand and hot sun of the desert. Abdul felt their sadness, and, besides, they were becoming irritable. Angry camels are not good companions.

One morning, Abdul knew that it was time to let them go. He thanked them for their kind service, and untied their hobbles. Before long they were out of sight. Abdul didn't mind. He walked lightly along a bubbling stream, stopping now and then to eat berries for breakfast.

Each day the sun shone more gently, and the nights grew warmer until Abdul didn't need his warm bedding anymore. When he saw his first waterfall, he couldn't believe his eyes. Flowers of every color grew around the pool at its bottom. As he climbed eagerly up the sides of the waterfall, he was not prepared for what he would see when he got to the top. Green mountains towered above him. Soft, puffy clouds drifted through the sky, and in the distance, waves washed softly onto a white sandy beach.

Creatures he had never seen before leaped playfully out of the water and splashed back into it, only to leap out of it again. Abdul thought he heard them laughing. In the distance, even larger creatures blew huge columns of water high into the air.

How could Abdul explain any of this to his friends in the desert? How could they understand him if he did?

As he marveled, the sound of laughter came floating toward him from a grove of trees. He had not heard that sound in a long time. At first he wasn't sure what to do. Then he suddenly began running toward the trees, laughing himself. He knew that something very exciting was about to happen.

Abdul had reached a special and wonderful place. This is what it feels like when you are doing your sacred task. Everything is new and exciting. You are happy. You wouldn't want to be anywhere else or doing anything else.

Your sacred task is part of the agreement that your soul made with the Universe before you were born. When you are doing it, you are happy and fulfilled. You know that you are in a special and wonderful place, like the one that Abdul reached. When you are not doing your sacred task, you are miserable. Then you are living in a desert, like the one that Abdul left.

Your sacred task might be to write books that help people open their hearts. It might be to start a business that supports the Earth. It might be to raise a family or become a carpenter. It might be to teach children or cook or sculpt marble. Whatever your sacred task is, you will feel very good inside when you are doing it, and you will feel very bad inside when you aren't. That is how you recognize what your sacred task is.

When you are doing what your soul wants you to do—your sacred task—nothing can keep you from feeling satisfied. That is the special and wonderful place. When you are not doing what your soul wants you to do, nothing can satisfy you. That is the desert.

To leave the desert, you have to follow your heart. That means giving up some things, as Abdul did. You might have to give up feeling that you are better than other people, or not as good as other people. You might have to give up seeing yourself as smarter than other people, or not as smart as other people. You might have to change things at work, or work somewhere else. You can always leave things as they are, and not give up or change anything. No one will blame you if you do, but you won't find the wonderful, special place that is waiting for you.

The longer you stay in the desert, the more you feel that you are not doing what you should be doing. Life in the desert seems empty, and not worth living. Nothing can make you happy in the desert. You don't have to stay in the desert. What would you rather do—bake in a desert or swim by a waterfall?

Your sacred task, following your heart, and creating authentic power—aligning your personality with your soul—all go together. When you align your personality with your soul, you naturally do what your soul wants you to do. That is your sacred task. When you do your sacred task, you are following your heart. When you are following your heart, you are in your special, wonderful place.

Aligning your personality with your soul doesn't happen just because you decide to do it. Abdul didn't get to his special, wonderful place just by deciding to leave the desert. He got there one step at a time. It took a lot of steps. Every time you set an intention to create harmony, cooperation, sharing, or reverence for Life, you take a step. That is how you leave the desert behind. The more you align your personality with your soul, the more you naturally do what your heart wants you to do. That is also what your soul wants you to do.

As you move toward your special and wonderful place—a life full of meaning and joy—you create authentic power. As you create authentic power, you move toward your special and wonderful place.

That is your sacred task.

Coming Home

I stopped in front of the small frame house. Kansas in August is humid, even in the evening. I grew up there. When I left, I never wanted to come back. Now I looked forward to returning—sometimes twice a year.

This time was different. As I sat in the car, a distant future seemed to form around me. In this future, my parents were long dead, and strangers lived in our house. They were wondering what I was doing.

If only Mom and Dad were still alive! I thought. Tears came to my eyes.

I looked at the house again. It was barren and cold.

If only I could knock on the door again. If only I could hear Mom say, "It's Gary! It's Gary!" as she hurried to open it.

Fireflies glowed in the dark yard.

I longed to feel my father's smile. I longed to hear him say, "Welcome home, Son!" as he joined my mother, walking slowly into the room.

My reverie was as painful as it was deep. It left me aching. There was so much I could have said, so much I could have done, so much I could have shared.

"Why didn't I see this when they were alive?" I cried. "Why?"

Suddenly my fantasy was over. I was sitting in a rented car in front of our house in Kansas on a sticky August night. My mother was alive. My father was alive. They were waiting for me. I opened the car door, walked to the porch, and knocked.

"It's Gary! It's Gary!" I heard Mom call excitedly to Dad. "He's here! He's here!"

The door opened, and there she was, radiant and smiling.

"Come here," she said, holding her arms out to me. "Give me a hug."

"Welcome home, Son!" My father walked slowly into the room. His smile was huge.

My prayer had been answered. I had one more chance. I held them, spoke with them, felt them, and let them feel me. My old room felt like home. I never liked it before. Even Dad's snoring sounded good. I used to hate it. Now I lay in my old bed, eyes open, listening to him gratefully. I was not going to waste my second chance. I savored each moment with my mother and my father. I listened to them. I talked to them. I asked them questions. I felt what I felt. I knew that I would never see them again the way that I saw them before, and I never have.

For the first time, I came home.

My fantasy made a big difference. It gave me a new perspective. Before it, I saw my parents the way that I did when I was growing up. I thought about my disagreements with my father. I thought about their struggles with each other. I thought about the things that I didn't like about them. After it, I thought about how much they had given to me. I thought about how important they were to me. I thought about how much I loved them.

The walk from my car to the porch was the same. My knock on the door was the same. Everything that I saw and did was the same, but my experience of everything was very different.

Becoming multisensory is like that. It gives you a new perspective. Things that used to seem ordinary appear special. You notice things that you didn't notice before, and you are grateful for them. Nothing seems accidental. Everything has a purpose, and that purpose is to help you grow spiritually. You begin to see differently from this new perspective, as I saw my mother and father differently.

You see the same news on the television. The same clerks help you at the store. The same person delivers the mail, but you see them differently. You appreciate them. Everything in your life becomes a miracle that is happening right in front of your eyes.

This is coming home in the Earth school. Nothing is ordinary, including you. You are still brown, black, white, yellow or red. You are still a male or a female. You are still from this country or that. You still have children to raise, bills to pay, and things to do. None of that changes, but you see it all differently. Your Earth suit is no longer the most important thing to you. Life is the most important thing to you. Everything you say, you say for Life. Everything you do, you do for Life.

You long for harmony, cooperation, sharing, and reverence for Life. You want to align your personality with your soul—to create authentic power. Your heart wants to guide you. Nonphysical Teachers reach out to help you. Responsible choice appears as a tool. A world of harmony, cooperation, sharing, and reverence for Life becomes your goal. The thought of this world calls to you, like the thought of coming home.

This world is the home that your soul wants you to live in. It is also the world that you were born to create.

Sooner or later, you will.

The only question for you to answer is when.

When will you create this world?

When will you come home?

When?

An Invitation

Dear Friend,

I invite you to join me as a spiritual partner in the vision of Genesis: The Foundation for the Universal Human. Genesis: The Foundation for the Universal Human is a new kind of nonprofit organization. Its vision is a world in which spiritual growth is the highest priority. All of its programs and projects are designed to support authentic empowerment, and to provide the experience of spiritual partnership—partnership between equals for the purpose of spiritual growth.

If you would like to know more about spiritual partnership with the vision of Genesis: The Foundation for the Universal Human, or to contact me, please visit www.universalhuman.org or write:

> Genesis: The Foundation for the Universal Human
> PO Box 1150
> Mt. Shasta CA 96067

You can also contact me at www.zukav.com

Share your soul stories

I would like to publish your soul stories, too. If you have a story that you would like me to consider, please tell me what concept in *Soul Stories* or *The Seat of the Soul* it illustrates. Then write it in less than one thousand five hundred words, and send it to:

> Soul Stories
> PO Box 1660
> Mt. Shasta CA 96067

I look forward to hearing from you.

Love,
Gary

About the Author

GARY ZUKAV is the author of *The Dancing Wu Li Masters: An Overview of the New Physics,* winner of The American Book Award for Science in 1979, and *The Seat of the Soul,* a *New York Times, USA Today, Los Angeles Times,* and *Publishers Weekly* #1 bestseller. His books have sold millions of copies, and are published in sixteen languages. He is a graduate of Harvard and a former U.S. Army Special Forces (Green Beret) officer with Vietnam service.

Gary's gentle humor, sensitivity, and deep insights have endeared him to millions of readers and listeners. His spiritual partner is Linda Francis. They lecture internationally and, through Genesis: The Foundation for the Universal Human, they offer retreats, programs, and other events supporting the experience of spiritual partnership. They live in northern California.